INVESTIGATIVE ACCOUNTING

INVESTIGATIVE ACCOUNTING

Techniques and Procedures for Determining
the Reality Behind the Financial Statements

Kalman A. Barson, CPA

VNR VAN NOSTRAND REINHOLD COMPANY
——————————————— New York

Copyright © 1986 by Van Nostrand Reinhold Company Inc.

Library of Congress Catalog Card Number: 85-7467
ISBN: 0-442-21163-5

Manufactured in the United States of America

Published by Van Nostrand Reinhold Company Inc.
115 Fifth Avenue
New York, New York 10003

Van Nostrand Reinhold Company Limited
Molly Millars Lane
Wokingham, Berkshire RG11 2PY, England

Van Nostrand Reinhold
480 La Trobe Street
Melbourne, Victoria 3000, Australia

Macmillan of Canada
Division of Canada Publishing Corporation
164 Commander Boulevard
Agincourt, Ontario M1S 3C7, Canada

15 14 13 12 11 10 9 8 7 6 5 4 3 2

Library of Congress Cataloging in Publication Data

Barson, Kalman A.
   Investigative accounting.

   Includes index.
   1. Accounting – United States.   2. Forensic accounting –
United States.   I. Title.
HF5616.U5B34   1985   363.2'565   85-7467
ISBN 0-442-21163-5

"A man's real possession is his memory. In nothing else is he rich, in nothing else is he poor."

— Alexander Smith

There are four very special people who, unfortunately, are not alive to have the pleasure of seeing their grandson in print. To

Colman Barson
my namesake, who I never knew

Abraham Cohen
with whom I spent many pleasureable
and educational Sabbaths

Esther Barson
a happy woman, whom visiting
was always a treat

Fannie Cohen
a wonderful, wise, and loving woman,
who will be missed as much as her
life was long.

In some way, everyone of them had a hand in this book.

PREFACE

This book originated from conversations the author had with his wife, Janet, which involved some of the intricacies and interesting aspects of investigative accounting. It seemed obvious during those discussions that this subject would make an enlightening accounting text. Also, the information garnered through various investigative assignments put the author in the position of being able to develop such a book. Interestingly enough, there was no book on the market entirely devoted to the field of investigative accounting.

The field of investigative accounting, also known as forensic accounting, has grown significantly in the past several years. This is largely due to the nature of our litigious society; the increase in the magnitude of awards; the amounts at risk in insurance situations; and the expanding of spousal (generally meaning women's) rights in divorce cases, especially in the area of equitable distribution. It is a rare accountant who hasn't, at some time, done some degree of investigative work, and it's a rare attorney or insurance company that hasn't used an accountant to do investigative work.

SCOPE OF THE WORK

Investigative accounting is commonly practiced in the following areas: matrimonial cases; partnership dissolutions (which is also what a matrimonial litigation situation is); minority stockholder suits; insurance claims (whether on behalf of the claimant or on behalf of the insurance company), as regularly practiced by the IRS; audits or inspections by corporate internal audit staffs, of various branches or divisions; and acquisitions or mergers. It has been our experience that the most common source of business for investigative accountants is through either attorneys or the courts in the matrimonial cases. Consequently, while much of what is discussed can be applied in virtually any type of investigative situation, the basis for most of the information comes from the matrimonial area.

The following are some examples of items discovered in our investigatory work, which put into perspective the wide range of this work:

- The boat expenses of children being run through the business.
- Checks payable to ABC Industries when, in reality, our work discovered that it was ABC Meat Industries, and that the expenses were all for personal food bills.
- Personal furniture, carpeting, and an alarm system paid by the business, capitalized and depreciated.
- Substantial bills payable to a local pharmacy where the inspection of the supporting documentation, obtained directly from the pharmacy, indicated that most of the expenses were for the sundries, gifts, and other non-drug items purchased for the personal benefit of the officer.
- The expensing of fixed assets through cost of goods sold, office supplies and maintenance accounts.
- Personal rent, utilities, and telephone expenses paid through the business.
- Nonrecurring leasehold abandonment expenses which, while legitimate expenses of the business, were nonrecurring and therefore, not reflective of what the business would normally be doing and should be expected to do in the future.
- Rapid or accelerated depreciation of luxury cars and long-lasting factory equipment resulting in overstated expenses and understated value of same.
- Real estate being carried on the books of a corporation at cost (proper accounting treatment, of course) which, in reality, had appreciated significantly.
- Frequent cash or petty cash checks written without documentation and for no apparent business reason.
- Payments to brokers and receipts from brokers, yet no reflection of market activity on the personal tax returns.
- Real estate tax deductions on the personal tax return that were for more than the home residence and other known real estate, which led to the discovery of additional real estate investments not previously revealed.
- Substantial medical reimbursement checks not deposited in any known bank accounts.

- No-show jobs for spouses, parents, children and paramours.
- A trucking company, whose volume of sales of its vehicles enabled us to extrapolate an approximate value of its existing operating fleet to assist in the evaluation process.
- A bar operation with a number of vending machines (including cigarettes, pinball machines, etc.), whose incomes were not being reported.

APPROACH TO THE WORK

Every effort has been made to be as clear and basic as possible, with no attempt at sophistry or elusive theoretical accounting concepts. This book uses a hands-on approach to assist the experienced accountant in very practical applications of basic accounting techniques. What should not be overlooked, is that to properly use this book, you must always be thinking. Investigative work is not a mechanical function — you must think about what you're doing; think about how to apply different approaches in different situations; understand what you're reading and seeing; and know where, how and if to take a shortcut. What makes this work interesting and, at the same time challenging, is that it is never the same from job to job.

Investigative work is seldom repetitious; that is, you walk into situations that you've never been in before, you're often viewed as an adversary (you are, in fact, often viewed with more hostility than even the IRS). Moreover, you must often work without the cooperation of business executives and have little opportunity to build up client rapport. Your work must be viewed as a one-time deal — you've got to understand what you're doing, do it efficiently, and do it well. As long as you don't allow yourself to become emotionally involved in the personalities of the parties, this can be a most satisfying segment of your work.

The approaches described herein are applicable to all forms of business organizations, namely, regular corporations (C), Subchapter S (S) corporations, professional businesses (incorporated or not), manufacturing, retail, wholesale, distribution, partnerships, sole proprietorships, and so forth. Some items discussed obviously don't apply in all cases (a stock register book has no relevance to a sole proprietorship), but the vast bulk of the investigative work is applicable to all business forms.

RANGE OF USERS

This book will be useful to a broad range of practitioners. These include:

1. All accountants, regardless of whether or not they perform investigative services.   The normal functioning of an accountant in understanding the business of his clients, mandates that at least the concepts covered in this book be used, applied, and understood.
2. All matrimonial attorneys and, perhaps, most business attorneys.   Attorneys, especially those who operate in the matrimonial sphere, will benefit greatly from understanding more about what is involved in investigating a business, and the services rendered by the professional accountant. Also, by understanding more of what's involved, attorneys will better understand what should be requested of the investigative accountant.
3. The internal Revenue Service (IRS) may find that its agents can benefit from this book.   Admittedly, the benefits to the IRS were not a consideration in writing this book, but they can't be overlooked.
4. Appraisers who wish to broaden their knowledge of investigative accounting, which is an integral part, and a precursor of the appraiser's ability to do his or her job.   After all, a business appraiser uses financial statements as a starting point, which in most investigative accounting situations, need to be restated or adjusted by the investigative accountant.
5. Judges should find that this book will enable them to understand more of the intricacies in a closely held business, and also where there is the need for investigative accountants. Moreover, it should enhance their ability to determine the accuracy of the books and records (and the income stated therefrom), the compensation received by the principals, and all other facets of the financial end of a business.
6. Internal auditors of corporations of all sizes should find this book useful in helping them to perform their functions better and to understand various areas where they might find irregularities within their divisions, subsidiaries, branches, etc.

7. Accounting instructors/professors and their students. While students most likely will not be in a position to effectively use the techniques described in this book until they have had at least one or two years of solid basic accounting exposure in the field, the insights that can be gleaned from various segments of this book will prove useful in the real business world. The polite, theoretical concepts that one learns in college — namely how accounting is used, the nobility of the double entry accounting system, the balancing of the books, the logicalness of the numbers derived, the extensions and postings, the profit and loss operations, etc. — are all very nice, but they should be viewed in a more practical perspective.

Although this book tries to be reasonably all encompassing, the author has no doubt that it cannot possibly be so. The practitioner will certainly run into circumstances that are not specifically delineated within the book; that's to be expected. The realities of the business world include subterfuge, deceptive accounting and tax practices, income hiding maneuvers, etc., which are as varied as the imaginations of the people and the types of businesses involved. Even in a lifetime, no one can expect to come across every possible situation, every type of business, or every type of experience. Thus, the most critical elements in this type of work are simply having eyes open; having the ability to think out a new situation (often from an adversarial position), and being able to think of appropriate business approaches on your feet.

KALMAN A. BARSON

ACKNOWLEDGMENTS

Besides the significant amount of work that I did to prepare this book, there are other people who warrant recognition and thanks for their help and contribution to the book.

First, to my wife, Janet, who, with the knowledge of over 15 years of marriage, knew how to encourage me to get the book done. Without her enthusiasm and eagerness to see my name in print, it is doubtful that this book would have come to fruition when it did. And extra thanks for her careful and thorough proofreading.

To my parents, Harry and Naomi, who saw to it that I grew up with a thirst and love for knowledge and a sense of fair play.

To my firm's support staff, headed by Eileen Mingle and Dorothy Stan, who both took a direct role in transcribing my voluminous dictation, and whose limitless patience helped me tackle this project. And to Dolores M. Schneider for her supreme efforts in the home stretch phase of the book's completion.

To Gary Skoloff, a contributing author, who was instrumental in getting me and my firm involved in this area, and whose constant affability has always been a delight.

To Jay Fishman, a business appraiser and character par excellence, with whom my association has been a source of constant professional reward, education and satisfaction.

To my seven partners — alphabetically: Sandy Freundlich, Frank Gatarz, Barry Kopp, Frank LaForgia, Alvin Levine, Dorvin Rosenberg and Nick Truglio — whose good humor and willingness to share the royalties of this project enabled me to get this transcribed in between innumerable financial statements and other correspondence. An extra thanks to Al Levine who, as managing partner, had the foresight to get the firm (particularly myself) involved in this area.

Finally, to my two little angels, Rebecca and Emily, who somehow got the idea that this book is going to be suitable bedtime reading for them.

CONTENTS

INVESTIGATIVE ACCOUNTING

1
CLIENT AND ATTORNEY RELATIONS

"My marks and scars I carry with me, to be a witness for me, that I have fought his battles who now will be my rewarder."

— John Bunyan

THE INTERVIEW AND CLIENT RELATIONS

Why An Interview

Clients pay you and thus, are the life-line of your business. How do you handle them in this nontraditional phase of accounting services? What's involved in meeting with and interviewing your client? What are some of the differences between this service and your commercial practice, and what are the procedures you should follow? Finally, what happens when you run into the impossible to handle client?

It is essential in investigative cases to interview, in depth, at least your client (if you are not hired by the court), and preferably all parties involved. Interviewing the wife (when representing her) is especially important where there has been a marriage of substantial duration and/or where the wife has been privy to the husband's business (particularly if the wife worked in that business or had knowledge of the goings on of the husband and/or his business). Of course, this applies just as well to the husband when the wife's business is being investigated. In most situations, the wife, no matter how uninvolved in the business or homebound she may be, does have some useful information to impart as to the husband's business associates, spending and other habits, hobbies, peccadillos, haunts, etc. You may obtain bits of information that will shed light on work that you will be doing later — giving meaning to names, places or events that you come across that might otherwise not have a meaning. As an example, the wife might know that the husband took his mistress on a vacation at a specific time and to a specific place. Upon your analysis of the business records, you might review documentation relating to a convention in the same place and at the same time. Or, if the husband's business is such that the purchases account can conceal many things, the wife's advice as to some jewelry that was purchased can give meaning to an otherwise nondescript item reviewed during your investigation.

An invaluable source of assistance (yet one of the least likely) that even the best of auditors would not likely equal, is the spouse or other litigant, who, in anticipating a divorce or suit, garners substantiated information for future litigation. It is even more unlikely that she/he would hire (secretly, of course) an accountant or an attorney for advice about future action and its requirements. Accepting this unfortunate fact, one of the first actions upon being called is to meet with the client.

Meeting with Your Client

In addition to accounting expertise, a good bedside technique is important. You must talk with your client, assuring her/him that she/he is part of a team — namely, the client, the attorney, the appraiser, and the accountant. Psychological attitude is vital. In keeping the clients' spirits and expectations up by explaining the situation and giving progress reports, we must be careful not to instill false hope that we are going to discover a hidden fortune, a bottomless well of cash funds, or a Pandora's Box of shady financial dealings. In most cases, the chances are that we will find something, although it may not necessarily be earthshaking.

After establishing a relationship with the client, we must use the client's knowledge as much as possible. During the initial conference, some points to raise and information to obtain (as applicable) include:

1. A broad perspective of lifestyle and habits.
2. The names of key people, especially those in a business relationship with either spouse or litigant.
3. Personal patterns — does the "adversary" travel a lot; entertain often; mix, or have the opportunity to mix, personal affairs with business; etc.?
4. The history of the business, to the extent either/both parties are aware of same.

5. How either party tends to invest, and with whom.
6. As much as possible about major expenditures in the past few years involving the personal lives of both parties, their house, and so forth. For example, did they take a $10,000 vacation in the last few years; was the wife given a mink coat; did they add an extension to their house; did they build a swimming pool; etc. Once you have a list of such things, you have another source of information of financial affairs that needs explanation and proof of the source of funds.
7. Anything else related to income, expenses, finances, etc. that is relevant to the purpose of your investigation.

It is best to conduct the interview(s) as soon as possible after being contacted. It serves a number of functions other than mere information gathering, that is, it gives the client(s) an opportunity to see you. That person-to-person contact is important because when things don't proceed as quickly as everyone hoped (virtually an inevitable situation), some of the client's hostility towards the adversary can be transferred to you. It is much easier to transfer that hostility to an unknown bookworm type, who the client knows only as a financial drain, than to someone the client has met with and established a personal rapport. It is also a good time to present your client with an engagement letter advising him/her of your fee structure (what can be expected from you and how you expect to be paid), and a good time to determine what your client expects of you.

Follow-Up and Other Contacts

As a general rule, it is a good idea to keep in frequent contact with your client. This is especially true for those clients who like to be kept informed virtually step-by-step. Frequent client contact is important from several standpoints: a consumer's right to know; your own ability to communicate with your client; your ability to collect your fee. (In some cases, clarify such contact with the attorney.) It may be desirable that you do not advise your client of all your actions, inasmuch as bitterness, and one party's lack of business knowledge and understanding of the advocacy position taken by the attorney, can cause her/him to jump to conclusions of grandiose results.

After you have done some of your work and developed questions and observations, try to interview the opposing side. Such an interview presupposes that you are representing one side or the other. The purpose of the interview is to understand as much as possible about the business, even if you discount some of what is said as prejudicial. Regardless of prejudices, the person who operates the business knows more about it than anyone else; therefore, questions should be asked about phases of the operation, its finances, sales, circumstances, etc. These questions should focus on anything that (1) needs clarification and rounds out your understanding of the business; (2) enables you to make a more complete, thorough, and effective report; and (3) strengthens your ability to testify and to withstand cross examination.

It is good policy to communicate as much as possible in writing (for documentation purposes), raising whatever questions you have, and resolving them. It is also advisable to enter in your diary a reminder to follow up all correspondence; you can't always rely on the other side to get back to you within a time frame that you find desirable. Effective use of your diary is a major key to efficient operation. Investigative accounting work requires constant follow-up and contact, especially with the side that you are not representing. You will most likely have to push to arrange meetings, get information, and obtain responses to your questions.

If you're representing the typical wife (in a divorce investigation), keep in mind that it will most likely be the first time in her adult life (or the first time in 10, 15, or 20 years) that she's going to have to file a tax return on her own. Most likely, she didn't have an income for a large number of years; never paid attention to such financial matters and, all of a sudden, is going to be faced with a tax return. Probably, it's going to be either as head of household or, perhaps, single — though it might be married filing separately, depending on the status of the pendente lite and other circumstances.

You should advise the wife that she might not be filing a return with her husband that year but rather might be filing on her own. In cases in which there are pendente lite payments, they represent alimony to her, are taxable to her, and there is no withholding against same. It is wise to prepare the wife for the eventuality of her own return, and for the possibility that she will incur a tax burden for which she might not be prepared, or for which no reserve of funds has been established.

The Dissatisfied Client

Notwithstanding all the right moves, precautions, and client aware-
ness, there will be times when you just can't satisfy a client; when,
no matter what you do, you're on the wrong end, and it's your
fault. Not too long ago, I was called in by an attorney to assist
him in representing the wife of a doctor. I should have been amply
forewarned when, upon our initial meeting, I was virtually grilled,
by the wife, as to my credentials. However, I merely attributed
it to a consumer's right to know, good naturedly answered various questions, and accepted the case, figuring that I had perhaps
a somewhat more difficult than average client to handle. (We've
all had that situation many times, whether it be in regular commercial practice or any special type of assignment.) Little did I
know.

Within a few months, the attorney who had brought me in was
fired and subsequently subjected to trumped up ethics charges; I
was then fired and mercilessly harangued; another attorney was
engaged and very quickly disengaged; and another accountant was
engaged. In due time, a few more attorneys came and went, and
my former client obtained a reputation through several counties
in New Jersey. It got so bad, she was even making semi-public
statements as to the varying degrees of incompetence of everyone
she had come across. As the new accountant conveyed to me in
apologizing for his client's misactions, it became embarrasing to be
still representing her. As a result, no one engaged by her received
payment in full, and whatever payments were received, to a degree,
were obtained by suit or lien. Fortunately, this case was truly an
exception.

Unless you're willing to sell your professionalism, swallow all
pride, and kowtow to an unreasonable client, there is nothing you
can do in a situation like the one mentioned above, other than dis-
engage yourself from the situation as quickly as possible. My future
has been tempered by this experience; the next time I get such an
uncomfortable feeling and the third degree, I will decline the case.

You have now been run through the basic steps in meeting with,
interviewing, and handling a client. After you have finished this
book, reread this section — it will serve you well as a refresher for
this vital element of your work.

ATTORNEY RELATIONS

Unless your investigative practice is such that your work is largely from the judiciary, or from insurance companies or the like, you will find that the vast bulk of it will come through referrals from attorneys. Thus, even more so than with your normal practice, it is essential to maintain excellent contacts and relationships with a number of attorneys. If you're fortunate enough to be in the good graces of a group of attorneys that does an extensive volume of such work, you'll have little need for a broad referral base.

Maintaining a presence and good relations includes such things as general promotion, relevant mailings, speaking before attorneys, and attending functions with attorneys. An aggressive practice requires that you use some degree of salesmanship with regular commercial clients and (because you cannot expect to get much in the form of client referrals in investigative work as you would normally get in regular commercial work) with referrers such as attorneys (the equivalent of the recurring client). This facet of your work should not be difficult at all in concept, inasmuch as many of the attorneys with whom you will come in contact are (like yourself) involved in service businesses; in general, of an entrepreneurial spirit; and of similar educational and professional background. In general, with the exception of your promotional efforts, whose direction is toward attorneys doing this type of work, there is little difference in the developmental aspects of this work from any other.

Initial Documentation Gathering and Follow-Up

In addition to obtaining the interrogatories, it is good practice to ask if there are any other documents that the attorney has that might be useful. A fair amount of confusion and duplication of effort (and antagonism) can be avoided by finding out if the attorney already has copies of three of the past years' tax returns; that is, there would be no need for you to ask for them from one of the litigants. Also, obtaining copies of whatever is in the attorney's file enables you to begin your work as soon and as informed as possible.

Just as it is important to keep in touch with your client, it is as important to keep in touch with the attorney with whom you are working. If you are representing both attorneys or the court, this policy is the same. Whoever you are working for should know where you stand as frequently as necessary. This is not to say that every time you get some correspondence or do an hour's worth of work, you must then correspond with every party concerned. For example, you advise/correspond when you make contact with the other side to establish the initial date; when you make your first visit (during which you get an idea of what to expect in terms of the condition and completeness of records and extent of cooperation you will receive); as you progress with the investigation, or as you meet with resistance, you must advise all parties of your progress and perhaps give an estimated completion date (with the usual caveats); as you approach completion, advise all parties as to a projected completion date. Frequent and regular contact will enhance the progress and success of any case, and will also give you a reputation for completeness and detail.

What Is Expected of You

It is critical to know what the attorney expects of you. Thus you must work closely with the attorney to clearly discern what type of report is required, what its depth should be, and what it should cover. Often overlooked in matrimonial work, but absolutely vital, is the depth of the attorney's knowledge in this area. Many attorneys handle divorces on an occasional basis and need expertise in the tax and equitable distribution areas. This is especially true for taxes, where attorneys often rely, and justifiably so, on the CPA to advise them and their clients on the tax options of handling alimony, support, and equitable distribution — both from the receiving and the giving ends, and both for pre-planning and subsequent situations. In working with the attorney, it is important to know if he/she expects just an investigation of a business, or a thorough analysis of the personal accounts of the individuals and a reconstruction of income. Many investigative approaches can be taken, and a job can be as simple as to investigate one bank account or as complex as a complete reconstruction of income for several years, estimates of lost profits or damages, a business valuation with a couple of alternative dates, analysis of brokerage accounts, personal bank statements, savings accounts and investments, and tax analyses and proposals.

Verification of the complaint or the date of the complaint should be obtained as soon as possible. (It is usually the sole date of concern as to equitable distribution.) Few things are as bad as presenting a report based on an inaccurate date. However, from a practical point of view, if the complaint date were, for example, February 20, and the business being investigated was on a calendar year, unless there was some outstanding event, positively or negatively, that occurred between the December 31 prior to the complaint date and February 20, it would be appropriate to use December 31. The mere passage of a month and a half, in most circumstances, would have no material bearing on your work. What it comes down to is that practicality must rule. It could be prohibitively expensive and/or time consuming to attempt to construct the financial operations of a month and a half or so (take the comparable period of the prior year(s) and reconstruct the annual results). It is also, in general, inappropriate to utilize less than a complete fiscal year of a business. Obviously, there must be a judgment made where, rather than only a month or so, the variation from the fiscal year is several months.

In many aspects of litigation support services, even though it is the client who pays you, it is the attorney who is your real client — the party with whom the continuity and the connection to future fees exists. Keep that in mind, and you'll appreciate the significance of this professional to professional relationship.

2
PRELIMINARY AND OVERVIEW CONCERNS

"It is a heart-rending delusion and a cruel snare to be paid for your work before you accomplish it."

—*Edmund Gosse*

"Getting it now is better than not getting it at all."

—*Kal Barson*

INITIAL AND GENERAL PROCEDURES

You have met with your client, been engaged, and had a discussion with your client's attorney. What must be done next? How soon do you start gathering and requesting records — and which records? How do you go about gaining access to the subject's business premises, and what precautions need to be taken that are not common to the normally genteel world of accounting? Do you use assistants, how do you best function, and what do you document? What other concerns do you have?

It is usually worthwhile to obtain a copy of the Preliminary Disclosure Statement, Case Information Statement (or equivalent); and the interrogatories, if existent, and review them prior to any investigatory work. These statements may give an overview of the situation, some insight as to what's going on, perhaps a key to certain things such as corporate or noncorporate business names to work with, personal budget requirements, bank accounts to expect to find and, if attached, tax returns and financial statements that would be useful to review prior to fieldwork. Don't take such documents at face — they are often self-serving and, not infrequently, evasive and incomplete in terms of the whole truth, nothing but the truth so help you.

Requesting Records And Access

As soon as possible after being engaged, send a letter requesting information and records to which you want access. This letter should be as specific as possible and based on whatever limited knowledge you have at the time, regarding the businesses and documentation involved. Don't make the letter into a gross shopping list — it loses its effectiveness when its length and scope are suitable for a company the size of Exxon, or for an individual with the business complexities of Howard Hughes. Make the letter to the point, reasonably all encompassing, and add a paragraph at the end stating what is obvious — that it can be expected that you will ask for more information if and when you discover the need for such. The idea is to set the groundwork for the basics so you can get started, and then request more when and if you discover that it is necessary. Refer to the Appendix for a sample letter that can be tailored to your specific needs.

The key step in physically getting into the investigation phase is to contact the appropriate party to arrange for an appointment to inspect the books and records, and whatever else is involved in the specific case. This is not as simple as it sounds. Depending on the circumstances of the particular case, you might have to contact either or both attorneys, the husband or wife directly, the controller, the office manager, the bookkeeper, or the other accountant. It is a good rule to document your calls on a control sheet, listing the date, the time, and to whom you spoke. It is rather common to get either a run around or a stall, and certainly, to meet with less than complete cooperation. This really should not be a surprise, inasmuch as, regardless of what you think you are doing in terms of a quality and impartial job, you are nevertheless viewed as the adversary in these cases. This often is the case even if you represent the court rather than a particular party. You are an intruder — depositing yourself on a business where its principal(s) would rather not have you at all. Keeping that in mind, you should be as diplomatic as possible so as to minimize whatever antagonism does exist, and so as to maximize your effectiveness in getting the information you want, and having the working conditions and availability of people that you need.

Once you have made the proper contact, it is not unusual to have to call again. Don't be shy — you must follow up these calls and repeatedly pursue the matter, with diplomacy. When you succeed in establishing a date, it is important to lay some ground rules (even over the phone) for the visit. Such an elementary item as the availability of workspace for you (and for an assistant) requires communication from the start. Double check that the other side is aware of exactly which records you need available. It is frustrating and wasteful to arrive at a company's office and ask for records, only to find that "Oh, we weren't aware — they are not available." Such visits serve no one, delay the case, antagonize both sides, and waste your time and your client's money.

Ensuring Access

Reconfirm your appointment two or three days in advance — remember, you are in an adversary situation. If you find you are getting stalled, having problems getting through to the right people, and not getting your calls returned, don't hesitate to contact the attorney with whom you are working, or the court, as the case may be. (Follow up in writing, sending copies to the attorney(s).) This is all part of the basic groundwork to document the steps you have taken to do your work.

If you have a problem with the date that you have arranged, if some unavoidable event occurs or whatever, give the other side as much notice and as much consideration as possible. Although we all recognize that in the business world things do occur at the last minute that prevent one from making an agreed appointment, you don't want to appear as the problem maker. Call immediately and even follow up the call in writing, and then arrange for a mutually convenient, new appointment. Basic good business practice — show up on time.

Use Of Support Staff

One of your first questions in establishing the parameters for your fieldwork is "Do I take a staff assistant along with me?" In some situations, you will be fortunate enough to receive, in advance, financial statements or tax returns, and also perhaps some insight as to the type of books maintained and the condition in which you might expect those books and supporting documents to be. If such information is favorable (i.e., the tax returns give you insight into where it is likely that it would pay to investigage and the books are in good condition), you may then be in a position to determine whether you can easily keep a staff person busy during your initial visit to the business location.

In determining whether to take a staff assistant along, one must also consider the experience and the skill level of the staff person. If it's someone with a few years' experience who understands what's going on, that person can probably keep busy without much guidance from you. On the other hand, if you're using somebody with perhaps a few months or a year's experience, whose function is mainly going to be bill vouching and schedule preparing, this type of staff person must have guidance. The need for such guidance will, in many situations, mandate that you have at least a couple of hours, if not as much as a half a day, by yourself at the subject company, to give you the opportunity to familiarize yourself with the books and records and to develop a workflow for your assistant. If there's any doubt in your mind, considering the normal time pressures in this type of an assignment, take an assistant along, even if that assistant has relatively little to do for a couple of hours. Such circumstances should be regarded as training situations, and the client should not be billed.

Work Habits

In setting up your workfolders and files, suggested sections include: interrogatories, business tax returns, business financial statements, personal tax returns, personal financial statements, correspondence (if the attorney you are working with is known to generate a lot of correspondence, you may decide that you want several correspondence files), a workpaper file for each fiscal year of each business (or a file for each business if more than one business and if each year is not too voluminous), report or statement file, agreements, appraisals, personal bank accounts, etc.

Document as much as possible. It is advisable, where there's anything that might be of consequence, to send off a brief written note and retain a copy. It is important that your correspondences do not take the form of an advocate arguing with his/her adversary. It is not always easy to remember, but it is a vital factor that, as accountants, we are not engaged to advocate. Our job is to attempt to arrive at a fair analysis of the situation. Therefore, it should not be our position to be argumentive, except where necessary to ferret out information. Your ability to get information, to conduct yourself in a professional manner, and to present your report to the court will be enhanced by your ability to remain dispassionate, independent, and unbiased.

Documentation will also improve your work flow and is, in concept, similar to what you would do for an audit. However, the verification tests and independent third party tests are somewhat different. The idea though, is that if you state that there are $40,000 of excess deposits in a bank account, you should be sure that you at least know the name of the bank and the account number. Your allegations must be as supportive as possible.

As accountants, we have been trained in good workpaper technique, which is just as important in these cases as in your regular work. You will have the dubious pleasure of being grilled on a piece of information — asked how did you come up with this, how did you calculate it, what is your basis for stating such, etc. It is much more professional, and personally satisfying, to be able to go quickly and efficiently to the appropriate workpapers, supporting schedules, and documentation, and to thereby clearly illustrate your point, rather than to thumb through workpapers and not be able to come up with an important item of substantiation.

Ensure Your Ability To Complete The Job

When you make telephone calls and correspond, follow up those calls and correspondence in a reasonably aggressive manner. You want to emphasize that you are being diligent in your efforts to get the information, to do your investigation, and to get the job completed. Also, you want to make sure that you do not make it easy for "the other side" to ignore your requests. This is especially important when representing the wife in the typical situation where there are time pressures, and time is on the side of the party that wants to stall. In most divorce cases, if either side would want to stall, it would most likely be the husband, who usually has the most to gain since he controls the money and is therefore in a position of less pressure and more flexibility. The wife typically needs the money and a settlement, and maybe is strapped for funds awaiting the ultimate outcome of the divorce proceedings. Therefore, it behooves you to keep the case moving. It is also important for you to show the attorney that you are a bulldog in terms of getting your work done — besides doing it right.

It is imperative that you obtain everything that has relevance to the job you're working on. This includes: selected (or all) bank statements, brokerage statements, financial statements, tax returns, reports, etc. Remember to get as much as you can as soon as you can, because the more you get initially, the less you are going to have to ask for in the future. In investigative cases, it is difficult to ask for reaccess to records. Once you have already looked at something, the reaction to a second request might be "Why should I allow that accountant to look at it again? He is antagonizing me; he's wasting time; he's creating havoc in my office; he's had it once, why does he need it again?" Such a reaction might carry some weight, stall the case, and certainly wouldn't look good for you. Therefore, upon first exposure to any piece of information, try to decide, before you leave that day, whether or not you want a copy of the information. If you are not allowed to copy it, at least you have tried. Of course, if you are not allowed to have copies, document this fact in the form of a memo and, if you feel it is significant, relay this information to the attorney(s).

Besides getting the year end financial statements, you might consider getting the interim reports, as they are sometimes more indicative of what the company is doing, and sometimes more informative. There are often significant differences between interim and year end reports. Some differences can be attributed to year end tax maneuvers, seasonal fluctuations, or various other reasons. Compare the interim reports to the relevant year ends, and get explanations for significant variations.

Address All Issues

Always compare financial statements to general ledgers to tax returns. Where the general ledger has not been posted for closing adjusting entries, use the accountant's workpapers to supplement the general ledger. The purpose of doing so is to find out if there are any financial versus tax differences and especially to highlight shady accounting practices — somewhat the equivalent of two sets of books. Any significant differences suggest areas that should be pursued thoroughly.

Keep in mind that one of the major aims of the investigative phase of analyzing the P and L (profit and loss) is to determine the true economic income of the principal(s). The tax legitimacy of an expenditure, that is, whether it is a legitimate tax deduction or not, is of no importance. The importance is whether an item is a true business expense or in some way represents an economic benefit to the principal(s).

Where there are related businesses, always trace the flows between the businesses and make sure the salaries, income flows, expenditures, and related transactions reconcile. For example, if a medical practice rents its office space from a real estate partnership (related party), verify that the rent is reasonable and that the rent money reaches the partnership.

Whenever possible, it is useful to obtain access to governmental reports. This would be especially significant when dealing with an establishment selling liquor or cigarettes, with trucking companies with ICC reports, etc. Governmental reports are additional pieces of documentation to correlate to the basic accounting records.

As early into your investigation as possible, get an on-location understanding of the money and paper flow of the subject company. Know who the key financial personnel are, who opens the mail and sees the money, who deposits the money, who records sales, and who controls the checkbook. This is standard audit internal control/procedures analysis. In an organization where there is a distinct division of duties, there is much less likelihood of unreported income.

It is not uncommon to have to deal with a partial year. For instance, you may be working on a June 30 date for a calendar year business. It may very well be too significant of a six month period to ignore and simply rely on the past full fiscal year. It may also be inappropriate to rely on the following end of the fiscal year — which would include six months of the year that is outside of the scope of your work. Therefore, it often becomes important to utilize a partial year. To do so properly, you should compare the vitals of that partial year with the same period of various prior years. For instance, are the sales rates approximately the same as those of the previous year (in which case your six month or partial year analysis may be of minor consequence), or has the gross profit percentage changed significantly? These are important questions and should not be ignored simply because you have less than a complete fiscal year with which to work.

Concerns On The Foreign Turf

Never allow the "opposition" to review your workpapers without your attorney's expressed consent. Your workpapers are your work product and, although they might be deemed "semi-public" in terms of their support for your report, they are certainly not until they have been formally presented. You are under no obligation to allow anyone to sit with you or look over your shoulder and go through your workpapers. Depending on your feel for the particular situation, it is recommended that you lock up your workpapers anytime you leave them (i.e. if you go out to lunch). I have personally found that it is usually sufficient to put my papers in my attaché — workpapers are rarely violated. Regardless, do not leave anything of a sensitive nature open for inspection by anyone, including your client. There may be speculations or notes in your workpapers that could be inflammatory or damaging, especially to a sensitive client.

In general, keep your eyes and ears open when doing your work at the subject company's location. There will be occasions when you will overhear or observe something that indicates that there is more that exists than meets the eyes, or something that will further support or explain something in which you are interested. For example, when we were investigating a medical practice, there was a question as to the ownership of a service partnership that we thought was related to this medical practice. While we were at the office location, we overheard a receptionist answering one of the phone lines in a manner that was not indicative of the medical practice but rather was indicative of the service company in question. Instead of saying "Hello, Doctor's office," the receptionist said the equivalent of "Hello, Lab office." That observation alone, indicated that there obviously was a tie-in between the two companies. That information enabled us to get access to the records of the lab and to include them in our report.

Mentally, there are significant differences in approach and attitude if you have the feeling that you are dealing with fraud, rather than merely investigating a business with the normal kinds of perks and mild executive abuse of corporate funds. When you get into the area of fraud the investigation takes on a nasty and more dogged posture. In such cases, you might put less emphasis on the disbursements of the company, basically the books and records, and be more concerned with the disposition of funds, the sales, and the unrecorded aspects of the business. Certainly, if you are investigating a cash business, whether it be a grocery store, a fast food operation, or a dental or psychiatric practice, your concern is cash — sales — not being recorded.

You must take a hardnosed approach, and concentrate on what might be the most fruitful area. (This is especially true if you have been advised up front by the client or attorney that fraud is suspected.)

When going out in the field on an investigative job, consider bringing your own table and chair. Use a portable folding aluminum or bridge table. You'll find that this may come in handy. I had just such a situation in a case involving a company that was giving me a lot of trouble. I suspected that since I was coming in with an assistant and therefore, needed two working areas, I might run into problems. You can imagine the surprise on the face of the (husband's) controller when, after confronting me with a lack of work surface, I went out to my car, brought in a table and chair, opened them up, sat down, and began working. It made an impression, helped me get the job done, and besides, I got a chuckle over it, at least to myself.

By now you should well realize this work, as interesting, diverse, and even exciting as it is, is far from the protective cocoon of a warm client relationship, once you step out into the field. You must have a firm grasp on what records you want, how you're going to go about getting them, and how to best protect your position in an, at times, hostile environment.

SHORTCUTTING

As with most phases of accounting, shortcutting is neither advisable nor desirable. However, in investigative accounting cases (especially when representing a client who is low on funds), where your analysis of the situation suggests that significant revelations and modifications to reported income, assets, and liabilities will not be forthcoming, judicious shortcutting is warranted.

Shortcutting obviously cannot be indiscriminate. You would not simply decide to overlook or eliminate your checking of various items without determining that it was appropriate to proceed that way. For instance, you perform your initial comparison of financial statements and tax returns. Presumably you find no differences other than perhaps, depreciation differences between financial and tax. Let's assume that these depreciation differences are not significant. You then go through the general ledger and determine which accounts seem to have the more significant postings in areas that would tend to lead to noteworthy discovery.

If, for example, you have a business that's grossing $500,000 a year, and the officer is pulling out a salary of $100,000, and the travel and entertainment amounts to $5,000, the odds are you would waste your time looking in that area. If even $3,000 or $4,000 of the $5,000 of T and E were personal, the effect on the company's operations and the income of the principal would be negligible.

There have been many times when the author has gone through the financial statements and general ledger and has seen an expense structure that was reasonable for the type of industry and the size of the business under investigation, and which would appear to offer little likelihood of personal use. Expenses were in line with expectations, did not vary significantly from year to year, and left little room for earthshaking discoveries. Therefore, I made a professional, experienced decision to omit various analysis steps as they were not cost justified. In certain situations, where you feel there is relatively little likelihood of finding anything, test checking, though still important, may be done sparingly. For example, you might only check one or two months of a few expenses, instead of three four months. You might further restrict the check in terms of the scope of what you will look at within those months — the dollar volume threshold that causes you to investigate further.

Gear Up For Accomplishment

The approach in analyzing expenses is to expedite the accomplishment of your work product. Indeed, anyone can go through the books and do a one hundred percent analysis of various areas, although this is rarely warranted (unless the numbers are significant). Also, from a practical point, exhaustive analysis will build up significant bills which, in this type of work, is easy enough to do — there's no need to do so with unnecessary work. You are also often representing someone who is not used to expenses commonly associated with business (your accounting fees), and you may find that over-analyzing (just as with an audit, where you overaudit) may result in fees that become uncollectible — antagonizing the client, the attorney and/or the court.

It is therefore advisable that, just as with an audit, you do some preliminary review of the operation in terms of looking through the general ledger or other appropriate financial records, and determine which expense areas are worth investigating and then, within those expense areas, which months are worth analyzing. As an example, in T and E (the classic category), presumably you've decided that it's an area worth investigating, and your review of the general ledger indicates (in a monthly posted general ledger) that three months of the year represent 50% of the T and E. It would make sense to analyze just those three months by putting the amounts from the general ledger on a worksheet, and then going to original source books and analyzing the substance of those general ledger postings. For instance, your analysis may take the form of a four-column sheet of paper, having perhaps anywhere from two, ten, or fifteen line items from the supporting original source books. You will then make a decision as to the specific items that warrant vouching.

Perhaps your analysis indicates an American Express bill for $37 (certainly not worth spending your time investigating), a travel agency bill for $2,645 (obviously, you look into this), an office supply bill for $78 (a misposting and a minor amount, and therefore, not worth checking), etc. The idea is that you make a decision based on your experience and your insight as to which areas and which specific items in those areas are worth analyzing. Even if you come across things that you are convinced are personal − for instance, a cash reimbursement to the principal of the business for $25 labelled carwashes, − when the amount is deminimus, it's not worth inquiring further. If you find a pattern of such types of expenses, which add up to a significant amount, then, of course, it would be incumbent upon you to do some further analysis. On the other hand, a few such items, without repetition and frequency, are negligible.

Use Common Sense

Generally, shortcutting is best achieved using both your common sense and your knowledge gained from experience. There will be many times when your first attempts at shortcutting highlight surprisingly substantial variances from expectations and, therefore, require a redirection of your efforts. For example, an area where you should avoid shortcutting, almost regardless of the expenses, is professional fees. Although the expenses reflected on the books might be more modest than what you would expect, a thorough analysis of these expenses might indicate expenditures for services performed in relation to a buy-sell agreement, a stockholder's suit, employment contracts, merger or acquisition negotiations, etc. Any of these might shed light on the financial activity of the company. They would also indicate, from an expense structure point of view, perhaps extraordinary items which should be discounted in the normal course of operations; and in terms of your assistance in the valuation process, a potentially vital element of recent activity that may have direct bearing on the value of the operation.

Shortcutting can be effective and appropriate. It must, however, be thoughtfully approached and utilized only where estimates, assumptions, and common sense will serve you well.

FEES

All niceties aside, a major concern for any of us in virtually any type of work is our fee, and its collection. This is even more so the case in typical investigatory work — especially in the matrimonial area. In other areas, in general, whichever side you're representing is involved in business, and either has the resources from that business or is used to the concept of fees relating to the business. In matrimonial work, when representing the spouse on the outs (generally the wife), that person often has no independent source of funds. Even when there is a reasonable source of funds for living, outside of support from the other spouse, there are rarely sufficient funds to pay for the unusual and expensive outside investigator accountant, who's costs typically range from a couple thousand to several thousands of dollars (sometimes in excess of ten thousand dollars), for the investigation of, typically, the husband's business.

There are a few general practices, which are always flexible and subject to variation under any and all circumstances, and to which we like to adhere. These practices are as follows.

Retainer

We always insist upon a *retainer*, with which we are comfortable — $500 does not cut it. Obviously, in matrimonial cases, there is little or no likelihood of a continuing business relationship of any magnitude. You will sometimes get a spouse as a tax return client, but that's not really a bread-and-butter situation. Consequently, it is imperative that the client appreciate, in advance, the expense of your services, and that money be received up front. There is no rule of how much money to request, but we would suggest that a reasonable amount should cover at least two man-days of partner service. For example, if you charge $100 an hour, figuring an eight-hour day, two man-days would be $1,600. A *minimum* retainer, therefore, should be $1,500 to $2,000.

Obviously, there will be times when you'll have to accept less of a retainer (than as figured above) if you're interested in taking the assignment, because the person you are representing just doesn't have the money. It then becomes a matter of a judgment as to whether you think your fees will be collectible (sometimes this means being patient and waiting). In these situations, it is imperative to look to the attorney, with whom you are working, for support. By maintaining a good relationship with the attorney, you will get support on your behalf, for whatever professional approaches are needed to obtain your fee.

Hourly Rates

It is our practice to charge fair, hourly fees and to also charge at a premium over our regular hourly rates. This practice of charging is appropriate in matrimonial cases, because you are not dealing with regular, or repeat clients, which means that you will not have much of an opportunity to recoup the usual new client, start-up expenses. Also, this type of work, as described previously, usually requires waiting longer than usual to collect your fee; thus you must charge at a higher rate (or charge interest) to make up the interest lost while waiting to collect. For example, if a year elapses between billing and collection, the billing is worth perhaps 15% less than when it was initially billed. Therefore, if your normal billing rate is $100 an hour, a 15% increment is necessary, which brings the rate to $115 an hour. This type of work also generates more aggravation and grief than do "routine" accounting services, and it is entirely reasonable to be compensated for the additional stress you endure.

Engagement Letter

Part and parcel with starting work in these types of cases is the preparation and submission of an engagement letter to the client(s). It is our practice, that every one of these assignments must have an engagement letter signed by the party or parties that we are representing, and that our engagement letter is almost always with the client and not with the attorney. From a practical point of view, it is the client who should be paying. If a problem developed on this assignment, such as the noncollectibility of your fee, you would certainly have a better chance collecting if the attorney were on line for the fee, although this is a very undesirable way of conducting business and maintaining a relationship. Also, the likelihood of continuing references from that attorney would be greatly reduced. It is also our experience that attorneys themselves strongly prefer that the client be on the line and sign the engagement letter.

Our two page engagement letter makes reference to mutual responsibilities, the general nature of our services, the amount of the retainer to be paid, the hourly rate of the partner in charge, the range of hourly rates for staff people, and other information regarding our payment expectations. We also have our inflation protection paragraph which provides that, after a certain date in time, the fees will increase either in a specified dollar or a percentage amount, so as to keep pace with a projection of inflation. We find that this is necessary in lieu of resubmitting an engagement letter, since cases often drag on for more than a year. You will find a sample copy of our engagement letter in the Appendix.

Collection

We strive for monthly collection of our fees — that is, within 20 to 30 days after our monthly billing. This is often not possible, however, especially when representing a party whose funds do not exist above and beyond the initial retainer. In such cases, you must accept this fact, at the onset of the assignment, and recognize that you will be building up a receivable that's going to take longer to collect than with your typical commercial clients. It is imperative that you understand and accept the realities of the finances in advance, since you're certainly not in a position to abruptly terminate or hold up your services midway, pending additional funds (which you had no reasonable reason to expect your client would be able to pay).

Once you've made a commitment in this field, and you begin your work, there is very little to report on, and very little product to show, until you've issued your report. An interim report, often oral, is usually of minor consequence, in that you haven't put the pieces together, nor completed all the phases of the investigation which much be coordinated to appreciate the whole picture. Consequently, except where you are not being treated fairly, you can not terminate services midway, — leaving a nonbusiness oriented person high and dry, and in dire need of your services.

In addition to waiting to collect your fees, you're also going to eat some of your fees in this work. Even though you've done the job and all the work is justified and documented (and no doubt it's been worthwhile to your client), the circumstances are such that your client just cannot afford to pay the total amount. In such cases, some compromising of the fee is often necessary — something that is not normal (we hope) with your typical commercial accounts. It should be clear to the reader at this stage that getting paid properly for this type of work involves a retainer, hourly rates, an engagement letter, and collection. All of these elements are crucial and require timely attention.

3
OTHER INITIAL MATTERS

"There are books of which the backs and covers are by far the best parts."

—Charles Dickens (Oliver Twist)

JOURNALS AND JOURNAL ENTRIES

The *disbursements journal* usually lends itself to easy perusal. Hence, you should briefly, but carefully, scan the column listing the payees, keeping an eye on the amount column and looking for large or unusual payments or payments to cash or to the officers. This is a step that is best taken after you've done a fair amount of account analysis, since having a feel for the books and what's going through various accounts, will better enable you to identify anything in the disbursements that has escaped your review, or that perhaps has been classified to other accounts or misclassified. Moreover, perusal of the disbursements journal will give you a better feel for the overall operation of the business.

It's important not to get carried away with this type of journal review. If you start listing every miniscule check to cash, or every payroll check to officers, or anything that to you seems unusual but really is normal in the context of the business, you're going to be spending a large amount of time totally unjustified resulting in nothing of any merit. Again, some initial review work to give you a feel for what is significant and noteworthy, will help you to use your time more efficiently and economically. Of course, there will be types of accounting systems that will not readily lend themselves to this analysis. In such cases, other steps must be taken.

Similar steps should be taken for cash receipts, which can be perused for nonsales items, or anything unusual or large coming from such sources as the officers or loans. Also, while it is preferable to go through the sales journal, there might be indications in the cash receipts journal of significant discounts or write-offs against receivables that might lead you to other questions — such as whether any discounts or write-offs are attributable to circumstances that might indicate that the amounts not realized by the company went "South."

In addition to vouching and analyzing postings to the various expense and balance sheet categories in the general ledger, we also find it very useful to review the *general journal* and *accountant's worksheets* (if applicable) for journal entries and other modifications. These entries are often of a significant nature, and the explanations accompanying these entries are often illuminating. There are times when such entries will clearly explain exactly what happened to various categories of expense and income, and enable you to more quickly understand what is behind various postings. In fact, in some categories, the only posting of any merit worth analyzing and vouching is the general journal entry. As with the disbursements journals, the receipts journals, the purchase journals, etc., it is necessary to analyze any and all of the books and records of a business to verify the legitimacy of various postings.

BUSINESS TAX RETURN ANALYSIS

When reviewing corporate returns (Forms 1120) be sure to include in your information gathering process the extent, if any, of carryforwards — net operating losses, investment tax credits, etc. These carryforwards may prove useful and valuable in the valuation process in that, depending on the circumstances, a loss corporation is of value to a potential acquirer. As the investigative accountant, you are the most likely person to have access to this type of information.

The investigation process at times is confronted with some rather unusual situations. For example, you may be investigating a person involved in partnerships or S corporations. In such situations, the income or loss flows, and often the cash distribution flows, are in proportion to ownership interests. It is not unheard of for someone with a bent for deception, to manufacture partners or coshareholders, in order to siphon off part of the income (or cash flow) to reflect an apparent reduced income level and/or to save taxes. However, this is certainly the exception to the rule. In such a situation, you might notice a flipflopping of ownership interests from year to year (especially where such maneuvering relates to the profitability of those years) even though there may be no legal and/or economic reality to the various partners and/or shareholders. Similarly, situations where there are partners or shareholders who seem to benefit disproportionately in comparison to their involvement (financial or time), might involve either artificial arrangements of ownership or perhaps ownership by a family member or a close friend with either tax avoidance, spouse avoidance, or other investor avoidance.

Always ask for copies of any tax examination reports for the last several years. While we are in no way bound by the IRS exams — whether favorable or not — an exam report often gives some insight into where the IRS determined there were problems. If no problems arose, the report is of somewhat less relevance, but it is an indication that an independent party looked at the business operation and didn't discover anything of note, concerning taxes. Inasmuch as our concerns go beyond taxes to the economics of the issue, and inasmuch as we're also concerned about nonrecurring (not simply nondeductible) items, an exam is only guidance — it is not the final word.

TAX FRAUD

Unfortunately, in some investigative cases we come across tax fraud. I am not referring simply to the frequent use of so-called perquisites or even to excessive perquisites, which are both common to almost any closely held business. I am referring to outright fraud, whether it be material skimming of sales/income right off the top, or whether it be grossly abusive, personal expenses running through the business. Upon discovering tax fraud, it is important to remember that your role is that of a privileged outsider, who is entitled to review the personal and business financial records of the parties involved. Your role is not that of an IRS agent (unless you happen to be an IRS agent reading this book), so it is not your responsibility (legally, ethically, or morally) to report those findings anywhere outside of the immediate group with whom you are working. Simply put, *you do not go to the prosecutor or the IRS with your findings.*

Tax fraud can be a very powerful leverage tool in negotiations and settlement. It should be noted that with few exceptions, proceedings in divorce court are in the public domain. That is, anyone (certainly the IRS) can obtain a transcript of the trial from the court, even if it includes potentially devastating testimony by an expert regarding tax fraud. Furthermore, in some jurisdictions, judges are under directives such that once they come across clear indications of tax fraud, they must submit their findings to the IRS or the prosecutor's office.

Use Caution

In a typical divorce case in which the couple has always filed joint tax returns, the use of tax fraud as a leverage tool must be wielded very carefully. That is, one must be sure by making threats that one is not endangering his/her own client. After all, there are many times when the "innocent" spouse will not (from a legal and tax point of view) qualify as an innocent spouse and will, therefore, be dragged along with the "guilty" spouse in any tax fraud situation. It is incumbent upon all parties to recognize that, when tax fraud becomes an issue, it is imperative to negotiate in good faith and settle the case as promptly as possible. Another worrisome factor in the discovery of tax fraud is that if the guilty party owns up to a substantial and perhaps devastating liability (even jail), your client (the innocent spouse) or the innocent minority stockholder will most likely be deprived of his or her one or major source of financial support.

It is important to couch one's terminology when addressing the issue of tax fraud. Unless your facts are well-founded, and unless you are absolutely certain about your discoveries, it is wiser to use euphemistic phrases such as "excessive use of perquisites," or "there is some question as to the legitimacy of the reported expenditures or reported income." However, if you are sure of your findings (the author has been in this situation a number of times), be explicit, either in your report, a cover letter, or both, and state that it is your opinion that there is clear evidence of tax fraud.

FINANCIAL STATEMENT ANALYSIS

Nonrecurring Situations

Be alert for nonrecurring, extraordinary, or nonoperational expenditures. Financial statements spread over a few year period may show significant differences from year to year. In certain years, there may be extraordinary items, whether income or expense, that tend to significantly distort that year in particular. For example, you're representing a plastics manufacturer that normally supplies industry or wholesalers with manufactured plastic goods and maintains a twelve percent gross profit. Under a special arrangement for a particular customer, the company manufactured a $500,000 piece of equipment on which it made a $150,000 profit. Certainly, this would seem to be an extraordinary item; however, it is possible that the company has always been capable of manufacturing the machine. Perhaps this one order was a harbinger of things to come and indicated a branching out of the operations of the company. Or perhaps the company, by devoting time, labor, and money to the production of the machine, passed up the opportunity to produce more of its usual plastic products and, therefore, the profit on the machine was merely a substitute for lost profits on its regular line. These are not simple points to address, but are significant in understanding the company.

Still another extraordinary circumstance that might distort expenses is a fire loss. Under most circumstances, fire loss is considered an extraordinary expense that should be removed from financial statements when making a comparison to other periods. Of course, fire loss is an unusual circumstance since it usually is not just an expense, but a loss of income as well; the magnitude of such loss is often speculative. Therefore, the best approach, if you're using several years for comparison, might be to eliminate that year entirely.

At times, prior year adjustments must be made. Such adjustments, if possible, should be reclassified to the year in which they belong rather than left in a subsequent year to distort that year. Sometimes, you must make a judgment as to whether the item is material enough or nonrecurring enough to truly consider it extraordinary.

We were involved in a case concerning a medical practice in which one of the physicians was buying out a former partner. Although this physician was generating a certain income, which had nothing to do with the former partner/physician, the practice was bearing the burden of buying out the former partner. We were never permitted access to the buy-out agreement, which had to be either a capital buy-out or a share of billings, or a compensation equivalent. Regardless of the type of agreement, the payments were being reflected as a deductible expense, the legitimacy of which was in doubt (but was not our concern). It was our position that this expense (occurring for only a short period of time) was not indicative of a normal operational expense of the practice; that is, once this expense stopped, the practice would still generate income, but without that expense as a burden. Consequently, it was our opinion that this expense was not a legitimate operational expense of the ongoing medical practice and, therefore, it was eliminated from the expense structure. Similarly, when the practice moved from one location to another, the consequent loss on the abandonment of some leasehold improvements was deemed nonrecurring and therefore, not indicative of an ongoing expense of the business.

Many times, the adjustments that you have determined, either in whole or in part, do not indicate any wrongdoings (such as personal expenses being paid through the business, or unreported income), but rather indicate that for whatever reasons, the business experienced unusual, atypical, and nonrecurring expenses. Our function includes not only determining if the officer is taking more out of the business than would appear on the surface (and if so, to what magnitude), but also includes determining the true and accurate operations and profitability of the company. If a company one year is laden with an extraordinary burden that is not expected to continue in the future, such a burden should be disregarded for presentation purposes or, at least, clearly highlighted so that the reader can appreciate the true profitability and operations of the company.

Examples of Nonrecurring Situations. Examples of these type of expenses include: the deductible (or nondeductible, but nevertheless deducted) buy-out of a former partner or shareholder (it must be determined whether or not the change in ownership by virtue of a loss of a partner or shareholder will have any future effect on the business' operations); moving expenses; leasehold abandonment expenses; large sales tax expenses (if a significant amount of equipment was purchased that was subject to sales tax, it is proper tax treatment to expense the sales tax — though from an accounting or continuing operational point of view, that sales tax is merely another facet of the acquisition of the asset and should be amortized over the life of the asset); unusual or atypical losses (or gains) on the disposal of assets; unusually heavy first year depreciation because of large asset acquisitions that utilize accelerated depreciation (especially if occurring towards the end of the fiscal year when the business hasn't had the opportunity to benefit from the ownership of such assets and their utilization and income production); and the write-off provisions under Code Section 179 for $5,000, $7,500, or $10,000 (assets that otherwise would have had to have been amortized over a number of years).

Of course, where accelerated depreciation is involved along with an adjustment to a particular year (to add back what was excessive in that year), it must be recognized that if there is economic reality to such depreciation, additional depreciation will need to be recognized in future years, thereby reducing the income of those future years.

Recurring Items Can Require Adjustment

This area can extend itself to expenses that are atypical (in magnitude or nature) of the type of business being investigated. For example, it is not unusual for a closely held business to rent its premises from a related party. Thus, the question must be raised, "Is it a fair rental?" This becomes especially important with the recent (1981) change in the tax law eliminating income tax rates above the 50 percent level. Business now has less incentive to understate its rent expense, thereby increasing its operational income and subsequently its salaries or earned income (vs. rental, which is unearned). With a 50 percent maximum tax rate, rents can be made more realistic, or even made considerably higher than necessary to help siphon off profits from a business — whether it be to mask a reasonable compensation issue or to deplete the company's resources and show a lower profit.

An example of another aspect of the rental issue comes from a medical practice that the author investigated. It involved the unusual situation of an incorporated medical practice owning the real estate in which it was operating. (Put aside the issue of the tax merit of this arrangement — it was already done.) Instead of rent, the medical practice was paying mortgage interest and amortization, real estate taxes, and was also incurring the depreciation expense for the building. To arrive at the true income and the fair value of the medical practice, we had to remove the real estate — which has no place in a medical practice. Therefore, we also had to remove the depreciation relating to the building, and the mortgage interest and real estate taxes. We then investigated to ascertain what a fair rental would be in the neighborhood for the amount of square footage, and incorporated that rental into the expense structure of the practice. It is vital to include such a rental; simply removing the real estate related expenses would leave you with a business without a rent expense.

Where business has worsened significantly in the past year or two, and especially where it doesn't seem to be in line with what you understand the industry trends to be, attempt to determine if the business decline can be attributable to a plan to affect the valuation and the income generation of the business in anticipation of a suit. Admittedly, this is farfetched in most cases, and very difficult to ascertain. But, if you can show, for example, that the officer is working significantly fewer hours, or that for apparently no reason the factory is on fewer shifts (while the industry in the area and in general has increased its volume) then perhaps you have zeroed in on a key item. Considerably more difficult to prove, for example, would be that cooperative customers have created a large backlog of orders awaiting a propitious time to surface; or that some business has been siphoned off by an otherwise unknown company with ties to the business you are investigating.

VALUATION

The CPA, based on wide ranging experience handling many business situations, is frequently well suited to determine the valuation of a business. This is often the case for service type businesses rather than for manufacturing, wholesale, or retail type businesses. Certainly, if you are one of the relatively few accountants who's had experience handling numerous buy and sell transactions and you specialize in a particular industry, then your unique insight into the operations of that industry may make you the most qualified individual to value such a business. However, it is more likely that you are not a specialist in that industry, and do not know as much as you should about the business (its past, its future, its industry, etc., and the macroeconomic factors that impact on it), and thus it is recommended that you urge all parties concerned to engage a qualified business appraiser.

In many cases, there is a reluctance to utilize more experts to avoid the appearance of bilking a client. Nevertheless, it is helpful to have, within reason and within fee ability, the best possible team available for the work to be done. From the CPA's point of view, it already has been determined that an investigative accountant is needed, so there will be plenty of work for the CPA. There is no reason to fear the engagement of another professional whose vocation is different. This field of work has room for many people, and there is money in this field to support both the investigative accountant and the business appraiser.

RELATED COMPANIES

A multitude of approaches and techniques can be utilized by the CPA, depending on the nature of the business investigated. We were involved in a suit in which there were multiple corporations, and a disgruntled minority stockholder with an interest in one of those corporations and no interest at all in various others. The other stockholders in the subject company had approximately proportionate positions in the other related companies. Our client was alleging misuse of corporate funds by other than arms length transactions between the companies. Inasmuch as he had no interest in the other companies, he was damaged if his allegations were true. On the other hand, inasmuch as the interests of the other stockholders in the other companies were in approximately the same proportion as in the subject company, they could only gain by being less than fair with one company to the benefit of the others.

In the situation described above, we found it useful to examine silo capacity. The nature of the business was such that it purchased fungible products, which were stored in silos owned by the company. Analysis of the purchase bills relating to silo capacity was made to determine if, at any time, the purchases (less, of course, any sales that would reduce the stock on hand) exceeded the silo capacity. Discovery of such would indicate that the product purchases of this company were diverted to other companies which had the capacity to use them. If such was the case, and if the diversion was not at arms length (the allegations included that items were being purchased by one company and handed over to another company without compensation), then something would have been seriously remiss.

MULTIPLE OPERATIONS OR DEPARTMENTS

Although most closely held businesses have only one real department or segment of the business, you will come across businesses with multiple operations or distinctly separate units, without which the company would still be or appear to be whole. This could make for an extremely interesting assignment. For instance, a plastics manufacturer that manufactures two kinds of plastic products is most likely one business, whose parts cannot be separated without risking serious adverse effects to the business. In contrast, however, a chain of retail stores, with five locations is, to some degree, five separate businesses.

It may be part of your job to determine whether or not that chain of retail stores would realize more income by eliminating one of the stores in the chain. That small chain of stores may have developed over a period of time, and perhaps some of the older stores are in what are now less than desirable neighborhoods, and have suffered economically because of that. Or perhaps, some of the more current stores are not just making it. It may very well be that the company would be better off without one or perhaps two of those locations. You must not lose sight, however, of the likelihood that even if a store, at the bottom line, appears to be generating a loss, in fact, that loss might only be after an overhead allocation. The real question as to the value of the store (putting aside the issue of its potential to divert management attention from other areas) is whether or not, after cost of goods sold and other direct expenses, the store is realizing a profit; that is, is it contributing to the overall business overhead.

Overhead Allocation

We have seen situations where one store, in a group of a few, shows a loss after various allocations. However, that store is contributing towards carrying the overhead — management, bookkeeping, etc. — and therefore, eliminating that store would merely shift the allocated portion of those nonvariable expenses to the other stores. Since there was a marginal contribution by the "losing" store, the entire company would be worse off without the "loser." But this analysis does get more difficult. Perhaps you are faced with a manufacturing operation with more than one plant, or a professional service business (such as accounting, law, or medicine) with a satellite office. With law and accounting practices, it is rarely clear as to what extent the satellite office generates business and assists in tending to existing or new clients at locations convenient to the client, thereby maintaining various client relationships. With a manufacturing operation, it is not as simple as dropping a store to eliminate a vestigial organ with no depressant effect on the rest of the company. Trimming a manufacturing operation could affect the sources of supply and the ability to ship out materials, could result in an overload on remaining segments of the operation, etc.

4
BALANCE SHEET-ASSETS

"Ah, take the Cash, and let the Credit go."

—Edward Fitzgerald

Remember that one of our aims is to assist in the restatement of the balance sheet at current market value. The historical balance sheet concept has little relevance to investigative work. If there is real estate, what is its current market value? If there are patents or copyrights, what are their expected lives and present value? If there is substantial machinery and equipment, what is it worth (obviously not the depreciated book value)? It is possible that you will not be professionally competent to make these decisions, although you will often be asked to express your gut feeling. You will, however, be in a position (based on your analysis of the balance sheet and general financial operations) to recommend the use of professional appraisers, who are competent within their own spheres of operation.

CASH

Basic to virtually all investigations is our concern with cash — the most liquid, the most meaningful, the most distributable, and the most capable of being manipulated asset. (This is especially true if we are dealing with a cash business.) The understanding, investigation, and analysis of cash includes tieing bank deposits to the receipt journals, checking out all bank accounts (whether they be checking, savings, or money market funds), reviewing cancelled checks as to their endorsements, and verifying that the checks, as written, agree to the disbursement journal. (In a partnership dissolution case, I discovered that the checks did not agree with the disbursement journal. There was a very good reason inasmuch as the checks were written to one of the two litigating partners and, as a consequence, were rather incriminating.) Checks made out to cash deserve extra scrutiny.   Adequate documentation supporting the business related function of such expenditures is often lacking. You must review bank account deposits, watch for where there are multiple bank accounts, reconcile the activity to the personal financial records, and be careful to treat nonincome deposits properly.

Bank Account Deposits

One critical phase of your analysis of the cash area of a business is the analysis of the deposits that go into the bank account. It is not sufficient to merely reconcile from datebooks or patient cards or journals to the general ledger and bank deposits. It is also important to be able to analyze the deposit slips themselves – the original hard copy type of entry record. Unfortunately, the deposit slips reflecting daily deposits are often difficult to obtain, because many banks no longer return them, nor do many businesses retain them. However, the bank records should be obtainable and should have detail that is comparable to the original. Of course, this can be a time consuming and expensive affair.

The purpose of analyzing deposit slips is to determine if cash is ever being deposited. It would certainly be unusual for most medical practices (i.e., general practice, family practice, psychiatry, plastic surgery, dentistry, etc.) to have income only in the form of checks (there are still many people who pay cash). Depending on the level of sophistication and complexity of the medical practice, and on the intent to deceive in the books, analyses of patient records or appointment books may not be sufficient to determine whether cash is being deposited. If there's a really sophisticated tax scam, such books will reflect only the deposits.

It is a reasonable and fair assumption that in most medical practices the absence of cash being deposited is a clear indication that cash is being pocketed. Other types of businesses where this would be the case are legal practices specializing in areas where the fees are often largely or totally nondeductible (such as some areas of litigation), or perhaps where the practices have an inordinate number of "mom and pop" type operations, which may be accustomed to dealing in cash; various types of sales companies in which there is a mixture of commercial/wholesale operation and individual/retail, where the latter may represent significant cash and the former payment by check.

Multiple Bank Accounts

Analysis in the area of cash requires a modicum of analyses of all cash accounts. This can present some interesting problems if you are investigating, for instance, a lawyer's practice. Just as you may expect a doctor to vigorously protest your right to look at his appointment book or patient ledger cards (alleging that it is an invasion of doctor-patient confidentiality), you may expect a similar reaction to any request to investigate the trust bank accounts of an attorney. Such an arguement, however probably carries less weight for an attorney than it does for a doctor with his patient ledger cards. At least with a doctor, you may discover, without intending to, the names of various patients (if you're dealing with a psychiatrist, this might be damaging) or perhaps, even procedures that were performed (if you're dealing with a plastic surgeon, this might be damaging). However, with an attorney, investigation of the trust account will usually disclose no more than merely the client's name and the amount paid — hardly, under most circumstances, a breach of lawyer-client confidentiality.

Reviewing trust accounts (in investigating a legal practice) is absolutely essential, especially if there are any intimations of fraud or unreported income. An investigation is necessary because, as is typical in many legal practices (especially the smaller, less formal ones), the trust account is never even reflected in the books of the law practice. The attitude or theory is that it is not practice money (and in theory it is not) and, therefore, there is no need to reflect the trust activity. Indeed, if everything is above board and nothing wrong is being done, there would ultimately be nothing wrong (from a financial point of view) with omitting the trust records from the main body of records of the firm. However, this concept, by itself, leaves the trust account open for the possibility that when a fee is earned and able to be removed from the trust account, and then deposited in the regular account, where it is available for disbursement for compensation or otherwise, the money might come directly out of the trust account to the attorney without ever being reported as income. Certainly, this is a fraudulent act, although in no way detrimental to the client (the lawyer is merely taking the money that he or she is entitled to, but not reporting it). Generally, if an investigation of the trust records reveals funds going directly to the attorney that were not reported as income (whether in the books of the firm or in some other format), it is clear evidence of fraud. The trust account is also a convenient and safe place to leave (significant) sums of earned fees to cause an inappropriate deferral of income from one year to another. Funds in a trust account are not reflected as income until withdrawn from the trust account and deposited in an operational account. Therein, the ability to intentionally delay the reporting of income and to cause distorted operations.

Upon investigating a business checking account(s), you might find that the company keeps unusually large balances. Unless there is a legitimate reason for doing so, (e.g., a credit line compensating balance situation) the company should keep less money in the checking account(s) and more in either a day-to-day savings account or a money market fund where it will obtain interest income. Since the late 1970's, the regular savings account has become passe because of its low yield. Money of any substantial nature that constitutes available funds should be maintained in a money market fund, or the equivalent, to generate a reasonable return.

Reconciling To Personal Accounts

Analyzing the cash phase of a business involves tieing the personal and business transactions and the financial flow together. An absolute must in your analysis is tracing the flow of cash — whether it be in the form of draw, salary, expense allowance, or whatever — from the known businesses to the known personal accounts of the individual; deposits, amounts, frequency, etc., must correlate. Reviewing the personal bank accounts of the principals is also extremely important in that at the very least, the personal bank accounts should reveal normal living expenses such as food, clothing, shelter, and pocket money. It is not unusual, however, (especially in a cash business) to come across a personal checking account that does not reveal much about normal living expenses. For instance, there may be no checks written for clothing or to stores, nor any checks made out to the person or to cash. This might suggest that cash is being taken out of the business, used for personal expenses, and not recorded; there is potential for a significant amount of income to go unrecorded. Or if, for example, you don't see any utility or telephone bills, it is almost certain that the business is paying such personal living needs.

Nonincome Deposits

Reviewing cash is not simply a matter of adding up the deposits in all the various accounts that an individual maintains, and comparing them to the known or reported income. In addition to nonincome deposits such as loans or tax refunds, there may be transfers between accounts and, therefore, a multiplicity of deposits that generate apparent cash flow but no cash. (This is especially true of anyone with complex financial dealings.) In one case I worked on involving a so-called entrepreneur type, he had at least a dozen checking and savings accounts, in addition to a money market fund, brokerage accounts and other accounts where money was going back and forth. Total deposits in any one year would run $300,000 to $400,000, while reported income was only $40,000. When I got through eliminating transfers between accounts, the result was $100,000 of apparent income from the $300,000 to $400,000 of deposits.

Often it is very hard to explain all deposits (especially when coming in a few years after the events). The key question is whether there is a pattern or a frequency of unexplained deposits. If there is an isolated deposit that cannot be explained and it isn't terribly significant, you most likely will have to pass on it; without something to latch onto, it would be a stretch to allege that it is unreported income.

An important factor (if applicable) when comparing deposits to reported income is withholding taxes. The deposit test must not include gross income but rather net income (after withholding) — that is all that is available for deposit. The timing of deposits is also important, though often it is merely that the individual was too busy or preoccupied to deposit his or her paycheck (or some other funds) and held it for a few days; or even a few weeks. Nevertheless, the merit of an explanation must be investigated.

If an explanation is dubious, it is not unheard of (if the case so warrants) to get authorization, signed by the person you are investigating, directing the bank(s) to supply you with copies of statements and cancelled checks for all accounts in that person's name or in joint names, for a several year period. Of course, this creates, in addition to an added expense, a delay inasmuch as it will easily take a couple of months to get these documents.

The analysis of cash requires a thorough review and understanding of the activity (and documentation) of all bank accounts, and their relation to personal financial records.

ACCOUNTS RECEIVABLE AND BAD DEBTS

The area of accounts receivable and bad debts must be investigated from a few points of view. First, accounts receivable has a direct tie to sales; that is, there should be some sensible relationship between receivables and sales, including that customers listed in the receivables are also reflected in sales, and vice versa. The omission of customers on either end might suggest an unusual circumstance. Obtain an aged accounts receivable schedule. Simply knowing the gross amount of receivables does not tell you how good they may or may not be. Certainly, if a high percentage of the receivables are noncurrent, it would suggest that perhaps there should be a significant discount allowed for the collectibility of same. Conversely, if an unusually high percentage are current, or from "blue chip" sources, it would suggest that those receivables are very good and have little need of a reserve for bad debts.

Industry Standards

Keep in mind the industry norm — some average low receivables and others average high receivables. You might expect a manufacturing operation to have perhaps 30 to 45 days or so of receivables — depending on the condition of the economy and the specific industry; and a service business might well run 60 to 90 days (or more). A company with a low number of days in receivables suggests good collection procedures and/or good customers. It might also suggest that sales have been low recently and that the company has caught up on its collections in part, by liquidating its receivables. It is also possible that the company is giving unusually generous discounts for prompt payment and, therefore, collecting its receivables faster. Such discounts, however, eat into a company's profitability (unless, of course, the company is getting higher than normal prices against which it can afford to give greater discounts, and/or it is effectively using the improved cash flow).

Related Parties

If any receivables are with related parties, the situation must be investigated in terms of the flow of funds and the volume of business between the parties. For instance, a minority stockholder suit, which the author handled, involved an auto dealership with significant receivables from officers and related companies. The minority stockholders I was representing were not active in the business, and had different interests in the auto dealership and the related companies, and had no interest at all in some of the companies. The intercompany receivables being carried by the auto dealership were uniformly one or two years old, and were carried without interest. As part of my report, I used an interest factor (at a fair current rate) for these receivables, which was reflected as income to the auto dealership. Furthermore, based on the available information it was determined that the receivables were collectible, since the companies were all operating profitably. Of course, had my investigation extended to the related companies (which it didn't), I would have reflected that accrued interest as a liability to those companies.

Understanding The Customers

Going through the receivables, just as going through the sales, can reveal a lot about a company's customers. That is, does the company have a lot of customers; does it have a few major customers; does it have major companies as its customers; are its customers local, regional, or nationwide; are its customers long-term or is there frequent turnover; are there contracts with any of these customers? A significant number of long-term contracts at a reasonably profitable level may have a value above and beyond any other value of the company.

In gaining an understanding of the accounts receivable, it might be determined that an intangible asset exists — the customer list. The fact that a company has customers, the right contacts, has established relationships, and knows who to contact to sell something, suggests that there might be a marketable value in the customer list. In fact, this is often an item in negotiations for the acquisition of a business, where it is stated in the contract of sale that one of the items being purchased is the customer/client list. Under virtually all circumstances, it is a good idea to get an indication of the number of accounts, the magnitude of some of the major ones, and the list of customers.

Bad Debts

Except to determine whether the magnitude of the reserve for bad debts is reasonable, there is usually little to be done by the investigative accountant in this area. Be careful to tread warily here – it may be rather presumptuous for you, a stranger, to appear on the scene and allege that the reserve is significantly overstated. The business's track record of several years' use of a certain percentage or method for determining its reserve (although possibly tax oriented) may be of substantial authority – too much for you to argue that it is not economically justified, unless you can convincingly establish otherwise. In addition, unless the distortion (overstatement or understatement) is substantial and the business growing, therefore increasing receivables, adjustment of the bad debt reserve account will usually impact only the balance sheet to any notable degree. Moreover, the effect on operations would be spread over a few/several years.

Understanding the area of accounts receivable and bad debts will give you a better grasp of the type of company with which you are dealing and also of its industry. For a full understanding you must address the issues of aging, industry expectations, dealings with related parties, and the reasonableness of a bad debt reserve.

INVENTORY AND WORK-IN-PROCESS

In a nonservice business, inventory is often one of the most crucial elements of the balance sheet. It is also likely, in terms of its relationship to the operations and the cost of goods sold, to be one of the most crucial items in the statement of operations and also to business profitability. (Note: Inventory also exists in service businesses.) Inventory must be understood and analyzed thoroughly. Thus, the following questions must be raised: How is inventory determined? Is it FIFO or LIFO? Is it lower of cost or present market (resale) value? Is it whatever gives the best tax result? Is it a gross profit percentage? Is it how much taxes we can afford to pay this year and still have a decent financial statement? Do financial statements and tax returns agree? Should you press for a current physical count? You may do arithmetic and common sense testing – is the stated inventory possible, reasonable, and in line with industry norms?

If the financial statements do not equal the tax returns, then inventory most certainly should be seriously reviewed. An accountant's report, even audited, may reflect a fiscal year (for instance; September 30), while the tax returns reflect a different year (i.e., the calendar year – December 31); and revealed are significant variations between the gross profit percentages. It is no surprise that the tax returns show a much lower gross profit percentage. This lower gross profit percentage virtually guarantees that the financial statements more accurately reflect the business operations than do the tax returns.

The potential for distortion in inventory makes for one of the most complicated phases of our work. Inventory's effect on the cost of goods sold in one year, will affect the following year. Thus, if inventory is understated at the end of one year, it is also understated at the beginning of the following year. Correcting the inventory to increase income for one year, depresses the income for the following year. Typically, a growing business's inventory adjustments will increase, and because of the cumulative increments in the inventory adjustments, the business will still show a consistent pattern of understating income from year to year.

If the job warrants – if it is rather complex and the money is there – it may pay to go to the extreme of actually conducting an inventory count, along with a complete reconstruction of the records, up to the time of that inventory. The importance of this inventory count, and what makes it expensive and unusual, is that the investigative work deals with a point in the past. You would have to reconstruct records up to the present point to make the numbers relevant to the investigation. Such a step would only be feasible in a large case with substantial dollars at stake, and would almost certainly require the court's sanction – no business would voluntarily submit to such a disruption.

Financial Testing of Inventories

One simple test of inventory veracity, which is useful in growth situations, is determining the adequacy of the inventory on hand (taking into account subsequent and near term acquisitions and sales, at a year end). If inventory is seriously understated (typically for tax reasons), it should be reasonably feasible (understanding the business operation and flows and the extent of mark-ups on inventory – this is absolutely crucial) to reconstruct the operations of a few weeks immediately following the year, in terms of the cost of goods sold. That is, to the ending inventory, add the purchases that occurred over the next few weeks. To this sum, subtract (*at cost value*) the inventory that was sold in the ensuing few weeks and, from that, determine if the alleged amount of inventory on hand was possible. For example, if inventory on hand was stated at $100,000 at the end of the year, and if, in the next two weeks, $50,000 of inventory (at cost) was purchased, but $200,000 of inventory (at cost) was sold (and understand that means shipped), there is obviously something wrong – you can't ship $200,000 of inventory if you've only got $150,000 worth (unless you've made a mistake in understanding how the business operates in terms of its ability to ship goods it may not have). Such a disparity between the number of dollars of inventory shipped and the number of dollars of available inventory usually indicates that the inventory was understated at the end of the year.

Another approach to test the veracity of the reported inventory examines the relationship between inventory and the space occupied (typically for a retail or wholesale operation). For example, assume you are dealing with a retail operation, whose floor space is 30,000 square feet, and whose reported (tax) inventory is $100,000. Understanding the nature of the product, and its relative density, it is obvious that the inventory (assuming we are not dealing with a date immediately subsequent to a drastic seasonal clearance) is insufficient to cover the business's needs and, pending further verification with other methods (such as a gross profit percentage test), is significantly understated.

Turnover

Among the numerous methods for reviewing the reasonableness of inventory, is to analyze inventory turnover, and compare it to expected or industry norms. It is important to know, of course, whether you are dealing with a FIFO or a LIFO inventory. In general, everything must be stated in FIFO to make these ratios meaningful and to maintain their comparativeness. If industry turnover should be five times a year, but your investigation shows 12 times a year, there is the possibility that the inventory is understated, resulting in an artificially inflated turnover rate. Although this is certainly not prima facie evidence of inventory understatement, it is an element to be considered in your analysis and investigation.

You might also analyze the time it takes for an order to pass through the pipelines of the business's sources into the business. Such an analysis might reveal that a business's scant inventory is due partly to easily accessible inventory sources with minimal lead time needed between the placement of an order and the receipt of same.

For tax reasons, it is not unusual for a business to continually carry an inventory cushion; in times of expansion, the cushion tends to expand. For instance, if your average inventory for the year is stated (because of tax considerations) at $250,000, but in reality was $300,000, and if your cost of goods sold was $2,000,000, your tax-based inventory would indicate an 8 fold turnover, when it was really a 6 2/3 fold turnover.

INVENTORIES IN SERVICE BUSINESSES

Most businesses that you will investigate have an inventory, regardless of whether they're on a cash basis or an accrual basis. However, sometimes the inventory is not what the IRS would consider an inventory — for example the inventory of a professional firm (legal, architectural, accounting, etc.); such inventory is known as *work-in-process*. Depending on the way it is structured and the way it bills its work product, a service organization usually carries a significant amount of work in process (unbilled services as opposed to billed services, which are receivables), regardless of whether on a cash or accrual basis. Also, especially where the work in process is large, it is wise to investigate the soundness of the customer (client) and/or the contracts that support such work. (There might be cost overruns which may make part of the work uncollectible.)

Depending on the nature of the practice, work in process can be extremely significant. For example, if investigating a law practice, it is critical that you know the type of work that the practice handles (general corporate, municipal, litigation, bankruptcy, etc.), its billing cycle and methodology of billing, what percentage of its work is contingency fee related or end result payment, etc. In certain types of legal work, payment is made at the completion of the services (except for perhaps an upfront retainer, which usually pales in comparison to the total magnitude of the job), sometimes several months to several years away. Thus, the present value of any such work-in-process and the collectibility for such work must be questioned. On the other hand, if a law practice does strictly corporate work, with little or no litigation or other types of one-shot deals, billings are typically done monthly, and payment is made within normal commercial time frames. In such cases, the work-in-process is usually not as significant — though it still may be substantial.

Although inventory exists in most businesses, it is the most difficult of all balance sheet items (with the exception of some intangibles), to value, and the most likely to be misstated.

PREPAID EXPENSES

Prepaid expenses closely relate to the related expense areas. For example, does the balance sheet show any prepaid insurance, prepaid taxes, or other prepaid expenses. Most businesses, whether cash or accrual, will have some form of asset that should be classified as a prepaid asset. You must review the major insurance policies to determine if they have been properly expensed, and if the prepaid portion at the balance sheet date has been properly stated. (This would be especially significant where a large policy was paid near the year end.) Similarly, as to prepaid taxes, you must check to see if there are any prepayments on the previous year's return or any subsequent interim prepayments towards an estimated tax. Many states require some form of estimated tax, whether it be paid at the onset of the year with the previous year's return, or as estimated installments during the year, against the current year's taxes. It is not uncommon for a business to just let these payments be expensed. Verify that the tax expense is correct as it applies to the current year's operations.

Another less common prepaid expense is for service contracts — usually not a major item. Maintenance contracts on such items as computers, copiers, typewriters, and registers might be paid towards the end of the year and expensed upon payment rather than reflected in part as a prepayment. Similarly, major purchase of office stationery and supplies (generally not major items and not easily discernible) may be justified as a prepayment, if there was a substantial payment for stationery and supplies towards the end of a fiscal year, and if it was expensed. This would certainly be an asset at year's end. Another prepaid expense might be the prepayment of interest (i.e., on a 90 day note and expensed on the books at the time of obtaining the note). Still other prepayments with which you must deal in your analysis of expense accounts, relate to rent, insurance, feed (if a farm operation), salaries, etc. Essentially, you are not merely reviewing what is in prepaid expenses, but you are also verifying what is *not* in prepaid expenses that *should* be.

Generally, adjusting prepaid expense categories affects the balance sheet only. The change in expense is usually substantially, or wholly, offset by a similar adjustment for the prior year and/or the following year. With this in mind, analysis of prepaid expenses is usually warranted for major items only, and where flagrant abuse is apparent.

FIXED ASSETS

When discussing fixed assets, you must keep in mind that this is an area with the potential for substantial revisions in reported income and net worth. If possible, try to get a visual feel for the physical operation; obtain a detailed listing of the assets from the accountant's depreciation worksheets. Then compare the listing to what you see. (Of course, this presupposes that you are working on location, and that you have access to all parts of the location.) For example, are physical plant assets reasonably accounted for in the listing or assets? Or, do you see much more than is accounted for on the depreciation schedules? If there is a need to inflate the financial statements for credit references, it is possible, although unlikely, for the assets listed on the schedules and financial statements to exceed the visible assets. It is more likely, however, (if there are any variances discernible) that the number of assets present will exceed the number carried on the books.

There are a number of explanations for variations in reported assets. For instance, internally manufactured assets that were never capitalized, but rather all related costs allowed to be expensed in the course of normal operations. This is not unusual for a manufacturing company where correcting the expensing of machinery can both increase the company's worth and reduce its expenses – thereby increasing its real profit. There might also be a substantial amount of assets that have been written off, because of past depreciation, and eliminated from the depreciation schedules. Though these assets might be older and, therefore, fully depreciated, their presence indicates that there might be a real value to them — one that should be taken into account. There also might have been assets acquired during an acquisition, a takeover, or close-out; these are likely to be on the books at very low values. Whatever the reason, the implication is that there is more to the company than what is represented on the statements.

You must get more information than you normally would for transportation assets such as cars, trucks, boats and planes; that is, serial, license plate, and registration numbers — and find out who is driving or piloting these items. (It is common for not merely a business car to be on the books, but also cars for family or a select friend.) When it comes to assets like airplanes, a decision must be made or a value judgment expressed as to whether that airplane serves a real business function. If it is in actuality for the personal pleasure and hobby/enjoyment of the individual, it would not be unreasonable to add back all the expenses of the airplane to the business to reflect those expenses as nonbusiness, items not necessary for the operation. Similarly, of course, for a boat. Care must be taken in general not to overreach by putting yourself in the place of management — inevitably, management knows more about running that business than you do.

Adjusting Depreciation

When you discover that certain items that should have been capitalized, were instead run through the business as expenses, and you make your adjustments to add back those items so the company cannot deduct them, keep in mind that you must also provide for a depreciation allowance on what you have now capitalized. If you allege that $5,000 of office furniture should not have been expensed through office supplies, but instead should have been capitalized, thereby increasing the reported income by $5,000, you should recognize that the business is entitled to depreciation on that furniture.

Your reconstruction of the P and L should reflect an allowance for that depreciation — not only for the year in which you are capitalizing what was expensed, but for any future years that are reflected in your report. For example, if you are doing a five year analysis and you come across such furniture in the first of the five years, the depreciation is most likely going to manifest itself in each of the years. This may (depending on what other discoveries you come across) actually reduce subsequent yearly income through depreciation that was not reflected in those years. Of course, you will have a significant impact on increasing the first year's income.

Valuing Equipment

When making an upward adjustment in fixed assets, it is important to remember that we accountants are not machinery appraisers/ experts. It's easy enough to allege that accelerated depreciation is a tax gimmick without economic justification, but do we know what is the real value of the equipment? Where the amounts and the complexity are substantial, a qualified machinery appraiser should be engaged. In more routine, smaller situations, an experienced CPA, judiciously using appropriate outside information sources, can probably arrive at a reasonably useful estimate of equipment market value.

PATENTS AND OTHER INTANGIBLES

Once you have ascertained the existence of a patent or a copyright, the determination of just what it is and its value is very difficult, and most likely out of the accountant's field of expertise. Many times a patent, if on the books at all, will be carried at a $1 value. The reason for the low value is that a patent is often obtained after a long period of work — the related costs are expensed and, therefore, not carried as an asset.

Where there is at least something carried as an asset, its existence is conspicuous and the investigation, though perhaps not easy, can proceed. Where there is nothing on the books and you have reason to believe that there should or might be, you must investigate related and supporting documentation (i.e., legal bills). For instance, a bill from a patent attorney would give you reason to suspect the existence of an intangible. Another source of documentation, although more difficult to gain access to, is the correspondence files.

If you determine that patents, copyrights, etc., do exist, you should recommend that outside experts evaluate them. Your function in this area would be to obtain as much financial and supporting data as possible, to facilitate the valuation.

OTHER ASSETS

A separate *petty cash* fund, whether it be a checking account or an imprest cash box, should be investigated; petty cash is frequently abused. In general, when investigating petty cash you have to be more tolerant of documentation requirements (i.e., accept slips of paper with initials that appear to be legitimate). However, there are many times when petty cash is a misused title, and is really another way of getting cash into the pocket of an officer without documentation of an expenditure. In such circumstances, it is reasonable to treat those undocumented expenses just as the IRS would — as money taken by the officer, or compensation to him or her.

Marketable securities, based on accounting standards, are typically carried at the lower of cost or market — certainly not necessarily indicative of what they are worth. Therefore, securities must be carefully analyzed and stated at fair market value, regardless of whether the market value is greater or less than the cost. Do not overlook the tax cost/benefit of the increase over/decrease from cost.

Security deposits normally is not an area that bears any fruit. It should be reviewed briefly to ensure that there is nothing of a nature that would suggest an option to purchase or some other esoteric type of asset that is not obvious on the balance sheet.

Deferred prepayment accounts, unamortized incorporation expense accounts, and other light activity accounts are usually of little or no consequence in investigative accounting.

5
BALANCE SHEET-LIABILITIES AND EQUITY

"If this were played upon a stage now, I could condemn it as an improbable fiction."

—Shakespeare (Twelfth-Night)

ACCOUNTS PAYABLE

To fully understand accounts payable, you must determine who are the company's suppliers and what the relationship is between the two. For example, if it was determined that a company relies heavily on one major supplier, the company's overall strength is questionable inasmuch as that one supplier would seem to have the power of life or death over the company. Of course, it may simply be that an established relationship exists between a company and a particular supplier but that there are many other companies with comparable products that could be substituted. Also, if one supplier is so valuable to a company, perhaps that supplier is a related entity — one that you should look into.

If a company's supplier was a major, publicly-held corporation, it would be rather absurd to investigate it. However, if a company relied on one major supplier that you had never heard of, or perhaps you knew of the supplier as a local company that was not very large, it is possible that there is some relationship between the two companies that might merit further investigation. In such instances, it is not unusual not to be given all the information that you have asked for. There could very well be other companies (some forming part of a controlled group) that have not been revealed to you.

Just as you would get an aging of receivables, payables should be aged to get an appreciation of the extent of the current versus noncurrent payables. If you find that there are substantial, old payables, a legitimate question is are these payables at all, or are they merely being carried on the books so that they are not written off and taken into income. If such is the case, there would again be a dual effect — first, writing off these payables would create income (which would have to be applied to the proper periods) and, second, this write-off would reduce liabilities, thus increasing the value of the company. You cannot assume that payables are not legitimately payable simply because they are old. There might be good reasons to carry them over a long period and, indeed, the company may still be liable for them.

LOANS AND EXCHANGES (SUSPENSE)

The loans and exchanges account is often a dumping ground, albeit temporary, for any number of odd items. Usually there is nothing of any real significance to your work in this account. However, it does warrant at least a brief review to get a feel for whether there is anything there that merits more attention. Typically, this account contains items that are either going out or have just come in, or other, usually minor, transactions that are expected to be cleared out (that is, no longer on the books) within a relatively short period of time, thus leaving no lasting imprint on the company.

OFFICER/SHAREHOLDER LOANS/NOTES PAYABLE/RECEIVABLE

Analysis of the flow between the officer and his or her business, regardless of the direction of the flow, and regardless of whether or not it goes through the P and L or the balance sheet, is a crucial phase of your work. We are not only concerned with what the disposition of money to the officer was and what the sources of funds into the corporation from the officer were, but also with the endorsements on the back of the checks payable to the officer. Also, if, for instance, your analysis highlights that the officer's loan account (in the form of a receivable to the business) is continually increasing, what you have is additional, unstated compensation to the recipient — there is often no intention of its being repaid. (Such a finding is important in its relationship to our investigative work, even if not in its significance to the IRS.)

More importantly, a loan account, by its activity, may lead the way to further significant discoveries. With funds flowing out of the corporation to the officer, the cancelled checks are to be inspected carefully to determine their disposition. Endorsements on the back of checks may bring other information to light. Also, the deposit of these checks might yield valuable bank account information — perhaps highlighting an account which you were not previously aware of. Your analysis may also reveal the use of funds by the officer that may suggest other involvements, investments, or financial activities.

If there is an indication of loans by the officer to the company, those funds had to come from some asset of the officer — typically, of course, from some form of a bank account or equivalent. (The source must be traced, and you must be satisfied that you have access to enough relevant information to that account or accounts.) Since allegations of a cash hoard usually do not stick, the source of the money must be determined. For instance, has the officer been showing sufficient income that would enable that kind of cash to build up? When tracing the flow of funds, it is vital that you schedule the information as specifically as possible, including the dates, to give credence to your work and meaning to your allegations.

Disguised Compensation

We have seen situations where items such as home mortgage payments, automobile loans, various cash needs, and checks for no specific reasons, were being paid through the business and charged to the officer's loan account. This is technically correct (from a tax standpoint) in that it doesn't get treated as a business expense; but money that is never paid back to the business nor expensed via a journal entry to officer's salary to wipe out the loan account constitutes additional compensation to the officer. The fact that it is not being picked up as compensation and as immediately taxable income is irrelevant.

Of course, there is an offset — the business is not being charged that expense, it is reflecting more income than it should. These are often tradeoffs. However, when it comes to questions about just what the principal is earning, especially where he or she is not the only or principal shareholder, and there are resultant allegations of a limited income source (the income being determined in part by others and, therefore, that person doesn't have a free hand to determine his or her own income), the use of a loan account may represent significant hidden income.

LOANS AND NOTES PAYABLE

The main thrust in analyzing loans and notes payable is to satisfy yourself that the loan proceeds were used for the business or, if not, how they were disposed of. For example, were they taken personally and, therefore, does this liability really not belong with the corporation. Or, perhaps, the loans were used for the purchase of various assets or outside investments or something else that should be reflected on the balance sheet that isn't, or at least, something that merits further attention.

Another point to consider, though not always the case, is that usually, when a company has a loan with a bank, it also has a banking relationship, and account(s), with that bank. Therefore, if an account in question has not been previously brought to light, the question is raised as to the possible existence of one. If there is denial but you have doubts, it should be insisted that you obtain authorization, under the signature of the individual you are investigating, for the bank to release to you any pertinent information. (I have done this before, and have found accounts that were either overlooked, forgotten, or denied for whatever reason.) This investigative approach is more commonly used where, rather than denying the existence of an account, no one bothered to keep, or admits to having kept, the bank statements.

Analysis of loans and notes payable may take at least two significantly different approaches – the analysis of the business and the analysis of the individual. Typically, a business has a full set of books. Therefore, an analysis of the loan account will not normally yield anything of major significance except, perhaps, if there is a long-term loan at bargain rates, or if loan proceeds or payments were for personal uses. The former is an element of value in that a loan at significantly below going rates represents a valuable asset – if the business needed to borrow comparable funds at the present time, it would not be able to obtain such favorable interest rates. Also, in terms of the continued operations of the business, a long-term, low interest rate is some degree of surety as to the business's continuing ability to keep itself adequately capitalized (if appropriate) at that present low interest rate.

An individual seldom keeps a set of books (journals and ledgers), as a business does. But an analysis of loans will indicate the flow and source of funds that relate to the liabilities of the individual. It will also, if a thorough analysis and confirmation of the loans is obtained, indicate the collateral, if any, behind the loans. This may reveal, in various instances, hidden or previously unreported assets. Knowledge of these assets and investigation thereof may lead to further discoveries of import, which may reveal, besides other assets, other sources of income.

OTHER LIABILITIES

The *payroll taxes withheld* account generally is of no consequence — except to the extent that it might be unreasonable. If the account has a very substantial credit balance, it may indicate that tax payments have been charged directly to expense and not properly allocated. If this were the case, correction of this improper charge would result in the reduction of a liability, an increase in the worth of the company, and a concomitant reduction of the expenses — an increase in income. It is also a possibility that this withholding account could have too small of a credit balance, or a debit balance. This might indicate that taxes as paid were posted entirely to the withholding account rather than a portion being allocated as an expense. This, of course, would have the opposite result as described above. Either way, it is your obligation to ensure that the account is properly stated.

Sales taxes payable are similar to payroll taxes withheld, as described previously, except that there is less likelihood of a significant misstatement. This account might warrant some adjustments (usually minor) due to returns or refunds; these normally won't have any real effect on the profit or the net worth of a company.

EQUITY

Normally, equity doesn't require much attention, because it remains unchanged from year to year. However, under certain circumstances, this area can be quite significant to an investigation. If the entity you are investigating had a recent infusion of capital (especially if it pertains to the person whom you are investigating), the importance of equity is heightened. Where did that money come from — this involves examining the records to satisfy yourself as to the source(s), the bank accounts involved, the history of those accounts, and the ability of the principal to come up with the cash (based on his or her known standard of living, income, and equity).

Even if the extent of your investigation is strictly the investigatory accounting phase (without your doing a business valuation), it is important to have all relevant information that is of significant import to the evaluator. For example, a recent sale may give significant input into current value. When transactions such as sales of equity occurred many years ago, however, they tend to lose their relevance and become of little or no significance to the current investigation and valuation. (Your main concern is the current business, not past history, which may not directly relate to the present.)

DIVIDENDS

We have found dividends to be the rare exception rather than anything remotely connected to the rule. When there are dividends paid in a closely-held corporation with multiple stockholders, and you are involved in a minority stockholder suit, it must be verified that dividends are paid pro rata — the same per share. Any deviation from this must only be in accordance with the class of stock one owns. In a minority stockholder suit in which we were involved, this wasn't the case — the dissident minority stockholder was actually getting less per share than certain other stockholders; this was something that easily could have been overlooked.

STOCK RECORD AND MINUTES BOOKS

In conjunction with the investigation of the stock record book (corporate business form only), it might be advisable for the attorney to file a request with the relevant state authorities for verification of ownership of the corporation. This is an uncommon step, but one which might be necessary where there is legitimate question about the real ownership of the corporation. There are many times when there are allegations that only a certain percentage is owned by the person whom you are investigating — and yet there are serious questions as to the veracity of such allegations. Also, when you suspect other corporations are involved, yet the ownership of these corporations is in doubt, the person you are investigating perhaps denies any interest in these corporations, and you have no access to records that might verify ownership, requesting information directly from the state is advised.

When there is treasury stock, it should be investigated thoroughly. Treasury stock indicates that the company bought back, from some stockholder, formerly outstanding stock. If the stock was of fairly recent vintage, and if it was a legitimate arms length situation, it may have significant bearing on the valuation of the company. Even if your engagement doesn't extend to valuation, obtaining relevant information will greatly facilitate someone else's work. Furthermore, it represents potentially useful and vital information.

The minutes book should always be reviewed. Many times, of course, in a closely held business, the minutes book is either not kept up to date (which is no great tragedy from an operational point of view), or if kept up to date, is little more than a self-serving statement of a couple of management's concerns, often as a protective device for tax purposes. However, there are times, especially when there are several stockholders, and especially when they have divergent interests and/or are not closely related, or where there are some differences between them, that the corporate minutes books may prove to have a wealth of relevant information. Most of the time, you will find nothing in the minutes books of significance to your investigation. What you might find, however, are changes in the way the company is operating, current events that may be of major significance, tax exam concerns, competitive issues, projections for the future, etc.

6
SALES AND GROSS PROFIT

"Books must be read as deliberately and reservedly as they were written."
—*Henry Thoreau*

SALES AND UNREPORTED INCOME

A company's sales is perhaps the area most worth investigating, especially when dealing with a cash business. When investigating sales you must acquire an overall appreciation of the business, an understanding of how sales are recorded, knowledge about the business's customers, and an understanding of the flow of funds.

Recording Sales

There are numerous ways to satisfy yourself that sales are being recorded properly. Compare the cash receipts journal to deposits per the checking account. Compare these items to any other journals or subsidiary ledgers. For instance, in a medical practice, it is very important to trace the day sheets to the deposit records, to the cash receipts journal, and to the general ledger and, from there, to the statements and tax returns. It is also useful to trace receipts back and tie them, on a random basis, both from patient record cards to the day records, and from the day records back to the patient record cards. If there is unreported income, you will at least have a chance to see it on a patient record card (which the doctor may keep for a number of reasons), even though it may not be on the day sheets. If you see a pattern of patient cards without the posting of payments for the services rendered, this strongly suggests unrecorded income.

One of the problems in gaining access to patient records is that doctors often argue that access to such records violates doctor-patient confidentiality. Whether or not the doctor succeeds depends on a number of factors, including how hard you press, how tenacious your attorney is, whether you have what appears to be reasonable financial justification for this request and, or course, what the judge's attitude is. It certainly doesn't hurt to ask a doctor for access to patient records — and you certainly are deficient in your procedures if you don't ask. In other fields, you might be asking for route cards, sales invoices, individual salesperson receipts and records, customer lists, or anything else appropriate for the particular industry.

Don't overlook the use of third party sources, besides banks, when you are attempting to get information. For example, you might ask suppliers of a business for documentation regarding the volume of the product that they sell to the investigated entity. Such documentation may indicate a volume that cannot be accounted for by the known sales.

Departmentalizing Sales

There will be times, especially when investigating a retail business, when it becomes very important, if reconstruction of sales and profitability is an issue, to be able to determine sales by category. For instance, if investigating a convenience food store operation, it might sell 30 or 40 major food items in addition to 100 or more miscellaneous and often convenience items, and these will have varying gross profit percentages. For instance, milk or bread might sell at a relatively modest gross profit, and a main product, whether it be a delicatessen or speciality product, might sell at a substantial gross profit.

It is important to be able to estimate sales by category to determine gross profit. In many cases, small businesses do not maintain the records from which such categories are made — or if they do maintain them, you will never know. It might be possible to categorize sales by analyzing purchases; by observing a number of days activities at random; by inspecting the stock on hand; by interviewing various knowledgeable people. When investigating a retail department store operation, you must address yourself to the differing profit percentages between clothing, toiletries, housewares, etc. Moreover, within each of these categories are varying elements that sell at differing gross profit percentages, to which you must address yourself.

Understanding The Physical Operation

In the sales area, if fraud is a concern, different perspectives and an intelligent look at the operation (not merely the books) are essential. If you are dealing with a department store, or some other form of business with a multidepartment or multicash register operation (and in some cases even with only one cash register), take a look around and count the number of departments, the number of registers, etc. Then, compare your figures to the figures recorded on company books and to the supporting documents to see if they correlate with each other. It is possible that an entire department's sales are unrecorded. You certainly wouldn't notice this unless you knew there was such a department. Indeed, all the other phases of the business and the related books might look very proper, and the omission of one segment of the operation perhaps not even noticeable. Moreover, one cash register might not be reported in its entirety or perhaps a tape of a day's or a week's operation of a register may not be reported.

Outside Collusion

One of the hardest items to discover in investigatory accounting is unreported income where there is collusion with an outsider. As with an audit situation in the typical commercial or nonprofit organization, collusion greatly complicates the auditor's ability to uncover fraud or defalcations. You must rely heavily on the veracity of external documentation and verification. When the external source is rigged, we are obviously getting back a false answer. Without anything to warn us of this bastardization of the accounting process, we are at a loss to refute the veracity of external sources, or even to suspect that the external information should be discounted or disregarded in the first place. We had such a case involving an importer of a food product, the price of which was known to fluctuate daily. The person being investigated, the owner of the business, had a very close and trusted friend in another state, who also happened to represent one of his major customers. The arrangement with this customer was that the invoices were prepared slightly below the going rate at the time of the sale, but not far enough below to stand out unless an exhaustive examination was done; however, there was also a back-up invoice for the difference. The money representing the difference, which was paid by the customer (close friend), was also withheld at the source by the customer and deposited in a bank account in that state, in the name of the person being investigated.

There is virtually no way to uncover such shenanigans, as described above, unless your suspicions are so strong that you do an exhaustive analysis of the situation. Upon doing an exhaustive analysis of the case described above, we uncovered that the same items sold on specific dates to various customers were always of the same price, except when it came to this one customer. We revealed a clear pattern of differences, individually of not very significant proportions, but considering the volume of transactions and the magnitude of each transaction, the differences added up to substantial sums of money. There was certainly the possibility of a sweetheart deal or contractual obligation that would make this a preferred customer entitled to a discount. However, there were no such contracts, and the wife did know that this customer was a close friend. She also had suspicions that there was unreported income. Consequently, we asked the attorney, through a contact in that other state, to conduct an investigation for any assets or bank accounts in the name of the investigated party. We started this with the bank with which the customer dealt, and hit paydirt immediately. What was discovered were CD's and bank accounts, in very substantial sums, which had accumulated over the years. Needless to say, the case proceeded smoothly thereafter, with no desire by the business owner to have the case go to court.

Medical Practices

Medical practices, if not favorite, are certainly one of the most frequent targets of investigative accountants. There are a number of approaches in terms of discovering unreported income, some of which I cover elsewhere in this book. For example, you (through your attorney) might "plant" a patient — one who is to pay in cash. This is also better if done with two or three such patients. Then, subpoena the doctor's records for the specific dates on which this patient was examined and paid for such services, and determine whether or not those services, paid in cash, were reflected in the cash receipts books, patient cards, patient ledger sheets, or whatever. Certainly, if the doctor being investigated is the type to pocket cash, this approach should prove fruitful.

The type of records and the business involved with a medical practice sometimes lends itself to the use of codes. For example, an investigation of a case of a couple of years ago involving a doctor who was strongly suspected of underreporting his income, revealed that next to numerous patient names in his payment records, there were dots and dashes. These appeared to be rather innocuous at first glance. However, upon further examination and analysis, it was discovered that, for instance, a dot indicated five dollars, whereas a dash ten dollars, of additional receipt — above and beyond what was recorded as received. The doctor's own records helped to hang him. Of course, the moral to this immoral story is that the paranoic need to know the magnitude of operations where you don't intend to report all, can prove to be your undoing. If one's ego is such that one has to have a record of what the real income is, that record can work against one in the wrong hands. If this doctor was satisfied to know that he was making considerably more than he was reporting, without knowing exactly how much, he may not have been discovered.

Use Common Sense

It should be recognized that there are times when a certain amount of common sense will help to support your findings. An example involved a medical practice for which we could discover nothing of any substance. This involved a dentist who for a couple of years in the late 1970s/early 1980s in his one-man, general practice, was grossing in excess of $200,000, and netting (salary plus retirement plan plus profit left in the practice) somewhat in excess of 50% of gross. The magnitude of his gross receipts indicated that, unless he was working an inordinate number of hours, he was in fact reporting substantially all his income.

There is a physical limitation to how much a one-person, general dentistry practice could gross in the area in which he operated. Furthermore, reflecting slightly better than 50% of his gross as net also was in line with expectations. While this is a common sense seat of the pants approach, by itself it is not sufficient. Our investigation of the practice indicated that cash was being regularly deposited in the bank account (we analyzed the deposit slips from the bank) and, further, that the living style and personal bank records supported the legitimacy of the reported income.

Furthermore, since a dental practice is not a unique business, we had within our own office, from our various clients, a substantial background of financial data from which to make valid comparisons between the reported operations of the dentist being investigated and our clients. All of our data tended to support, beyond any reasonable doubt, that to all material and substantial effects, the dentist was re-porting his income properly. This is not to say that he wasn't per-haps pocketing a few thousand dollars — but that was not material, considering his admitted income was in excess of $100,000 per year.

From a practical point of view, such minimal pocketing of income (as described above) is not discoverable without exhaustive and prohibi-tively expensive investigation. It's similar to the concept of a bank rec-onciliation, where you've done the work diligently, and you find that you're off 10¢ in a business where the volume going through the check-ing account is several thousand dollars. In such a case, the effort to dis-cover the 10¢ error is just not cost justified, nor is it reasonable in light of its magnitude.

Restaurants

If investigating a restaurant business, a consideration should be the linen or laundry bills. If you were to take all the linen bills for a consec-utive two month period, analyze the number of tablecloths laundered, take into account the size of the tablecloths (larger tables require larger tablecloths and have more people at them), and from that information, develop a profile of the magnitude of the volume of the business in terms of the number of people that were likely served within a period of time (and obviously leave room for a margin of error — i.e., a table-cloth suitable for a table for four might have been used by two people), and then further expand upon that by using industry norms (or individ-ually developed averages for that specific restaurant) as to what the average bill is (keeping in mind, for instance, that dinner bills are more than lunch bills, which are more than breakfast bills), you may arrive at a very viable method for reconstructing the income of that restaurant. This method, since it has numerous areas of impreciseness and inexact-ness, and since various assumptions must be made, should be utilized over two or three different periods of time. If your findings are fairly consistent as to the magnitude of unreported income during each of those periods of time, then you've developed all the more support for your approach. If, on the other hand, you find inconsistencies, you'll obviously need to take a second or third hard look at what you've done, reevaluate your approaches, and perhaps even discard the whole approach if you can't establish a pattern of unreported income. The concept here is that if an individual is inclined to pocket cash, he or she will do so on a fairly consistent basis, even though there might be fluctuations between the periods of time that the cash is pocketed. If you can't show a consistent pattern of cash pocketing, then either there is no pocketing of income, or your approach is remiss. The discovery that cash might have been pocketed once (or perhaps for one month or one specific period of time) is nowhere near as meaningful or believable than if it was consistently pocketed over a few test periods.

An approach similar to the one outlined above (with certain advantages), is to count the number of placemats used. One problem with tablecloths is that many restaurants, especially diners, don't use tablecloths — they have hard metal or formica tops that are wiped clean after each use, and no tablecloth is needed. On the other hand, many restaurants that don't use tablecloths use placemats. Most use paper or disposable placemats, which are purchased in large numbers. Therefore, it's important to do your test check over a more lengthy period of time than you would for tablecloths. If you cut your test period too soon, you'll have a grossly distorted view as to the number of placemats used in that time frame.

The approach for placemats is similar to the approach for tablecloths — the number of placemats used should be a fair indication of the number of meals served. In fact, the number of placemats used is perhaps more closely aligned to the number of meals served than is the number of tablecloths laundered. More specifically, whereas two people might use a tablecloth suitable for four, or four people might use a tablecloth suitable for eight, a placemat is most likely used by one person. You would still need room for a margin of error — sometimes a table for four is used by two people who then use up an extra placemat, or placemats (being disposable) are sometimes discarded if there's a rip in them. Nevertheless, there is and should be expected to be, after an allowance for a margin of error, a close relationship between the number of placements used and the number of meals served.

Other Businesses

The Oldest Profession. One of the classic investigations of a cash business is the reputed investigation by the Internal Revenue Service of a whorehouse, which until recently, was the archetypical cash business. In analyzing the income of such a business, keep in mind that there is no such thing as a gross profit percentage to use and, most likely, no meaningful records to utilize. The rumor is that some unsung hero got the brilliant idea of analyzing the laundry bills of the whorehouse to determine the number of towels that were washed. Fortunately, this whorehouse didn't have an internal laundry system, and had to rely on the outside. Calculating one john per towel (with a slight allowance for non-john use of towels), it was possible to determine the number of johns serviced over a period of time. Then, utilizing the going rate per john (allowing for additional fees for variations) the investigator was able to accurately (?) reconstruct the house's income. The method is ingenious, classical (from an investigative point of view), and most reliable.

School Days. Perhaps you're investigating a school — obviously not a public school, but a private school (accredited, full-time private school, or an after school hours dance academy, a gymnastics school, an art school, or whatever). Some of these schools, especially those whose payments are nondeductible, are paid in cash. To analyze the income you might, for instance, call up the school and ask what the tuition is and perhaps, what the number of students in the school is — a question that a concerned prospective parent or student would likely ask. You might subpoena or otherwise get access to records to discover the number of students in each class (different classes sometimes have different tuition rates) and from that, reconstruct a profile of the school in terms of the number of students, the tuition rates, and the gross income. An important point to note here is that sometimes something as simple as a phone call or looking in the yellow pages of the telephone book, can be extremely fruitful.

Grass Roots Retail. Approaches necessary to reconstruct income can vary substantially with the particular circumstances. One of the more interesting situations that the author was involved in was the reconstruction of the income of a flea market. It was owned and run by one of the parties being investigated. There were allegations that, especially since it was a cash business, there was unreported income. We had a reasonable and decent set of books with which to work. However, it would have been no great effort for various cash receipt items not to have been included in the books at all. To reconstruct the income, we had one of our staff people go the the flea market on three different Saturdays and Sundays when the weather was favorable, and on each of those days, count the number of tables that were being used (being rented by the flea market owner/manager). (It should be noted that this flea market was open only on Saturdays and Sundays.) We also checked weather bureau records of past weekend weather to determine which days the flea market should have been open. Of course, we had to take into account holiday weekends (Easter Sunday is not a big flea market day, and on Christmas, almost all flea markets are closed). This gathering of information helped us to reconstruct the magnitude of the income of the flea market and, in fact, determine that there was an understatement of income.

Other Concerns

It would certainly be significant if you were to find out that a major portion of the sales of the company comes from one or a few customers. That puts the company in a more tenuous position. Also, the investigation of sales can uncover long-term sales contracts. Such contracts, medium or long-term, would certainly indicate a strong company. The absence of long-term contracts would be detrimental in an industry where contracts were the norm.

Sometimes, the existence of one thing leads you to believe, or discover, the existence of another. For example, if there are allegations of unreported income, and your investigative work discloses that there is, for instance, a slush fund used to pay off inspectors or finders of business, or that there are employees paid in cash, then it is reasonable to expect that cash (unreported income or phony deductions) is also being used to compensate the officer or owner of the business. If cash is available for one or two types of expenses (slush fund or payroll), then certainly it should be available for another type of an expense — officer/owner compensation. This, by the way, does not make those cash expenses any less a legitimate business expense then if they were paid by check or on the books. These expenses, nowithstanding the potential for serious tax and legal problems, are legitimate business expenses when paid for services rendered or other real business needs.

Sales, and the determination of whether or not they are recorded, is a crucial element of our work. Each type of business has its own peculiararities thus requiring the understanding of funds flow, sales, bookkeeping procedures, and operations of the business. Your ability to think of creative ways to test the veracity of reported sales will often determine the degree of your success you realize.

GROSS PROFIT/COST OF GOODS SOLD

One general approach when analyzing the sales operation, especially when it is not in line with what you think it should be, is that a gross profit, or cost of goods sold test, may be of great help. If a reasonably broad and representative analysis of the cost of goods were made (understanding the business's operations), there should be some reasonably close correlation between your sample percentages and those reported by the business in its books and records, financial statements, and tax returns.

Gross Profit As A Key Indicator

In some cases, your strongest indication of unreported income can be obtained with a gross profit test. (Of course, this is applicable only for some businesses.) Many businesses have a fairly narrow range for their gross profit percentage standard (an indication of what the business should be doing). If the business being investigated is one of those businesses, and the gross profit is considerably less than the standard gross profit, and if there are no justifiable reasons (such as local competition, particular product mix, neighborhood conditions, or whatever), then unreported income may exist. To hinge your report and allegations of unreported income on gross profit calculations, you have to have a situation with significant distortions (variations from the norm). A couple of percentage points, unless concerned with a high volume and a tightly controlled industry, is normally just too narrow of a gap to be able to state that unreported income exists and to make the allegation stick.

Gross Profit — Retail Food

In the investigation of a retail food store operation, though the books were fairly clean, the deposits to the personal accounts strongly indicated that there was a material understatement of income. That, by itself, would probably have been sufficient to establish unreported sales, additional income to the business and the individual, and probably even tax fraud (though of course the investigative accountant's role, unless representing the IRS, is not to create a case for tax fraud). However, it was deemed necessary and useful to be able to prove the unreported income in another fashion so as to further support the bank deposits and life style evidenced in the personal accounts of the individual, and also to further and more specifically quantify the extent of unreported income. This was done by taking a sampling of the business's more typical and popular sales items — determined by simply asking questions, taking a walk around the store, and jotting down various items and their current sales prices. Then, inspection of the current purchase invoices was done for those same items, and the costs and their corresponding percentages were determined. To balance this analysis, it was also important to reflect shrinkage or loss (i.e., certain foods shrink upon cooking or experience trimming losses upon cutting and selling to the public). The resultant comparison of costs to sales price developed a very usable and supportable gross profit percentage. This approach helped to further prove that income was underreported by substantial amounts.

It is important to note that in the investigation described above, current sales prices and current purchase prices were utilized. The reason is that, unless the business had unusually good records in terms of old (one, two, or three years old) sales prices, you have available with which to work only the current numbers, the ones that you can experience at the time you are there. This is another strong indication of why it is essential that you do at least some of your work on the premises of the business that you are investigating. Provided that no radical change has occurred in the last few years (that is, from your current use of current numbers vs. your financial analysis for the past couple of years), this approach is most valid.

Gross Profit — Used Cars

Another relevant case involved a used car dealership, whose gross profit percentages were far below industry norms. That, by itself, suggested something was not proper — though, by itself, was only sufficient for intimations, certainly not strong enough to make accusations. Furthermore, the individual's bank records were in inadequate condition, such that life style could not be determined, and there were strong indications that a good deal of the alleged unreported income was retained in the form of cash, never seeing the daylight of a bank account.

The approach utilized for this used car dealership was to take three months of sales invoices, and thoroughly analyze them as to sales price vs. cost, with the resultant computation of gross profit. Fortunately, the business maintained a card for each car indicating costs and additional expenses (such as reconditioning and other repairs that went into the cost of goods sold) thus enabling this comparison. This analysis showed a consistent pattern of gross profit percentages a few points higher than that reflected in the company's financial statements and tax returns. Considering that the business was doing in excess of $2,000,000 in sales, a few percentage points represented potentially $50,000 to $100,000 of unreported income. This approach was most useful and credible — simply knowing that the reported gross profit was below industry norms is insufficient when there is the possibility that the business has a mix of cars that doesn't permit it to realize industry norms.

Overview

An analysis of the cost of goods sold (in the sense of a review of disbursements as would be done with any other expense account), although not generally revealing anything surprising or unusual, is sometimes a gold mine of interesting information. Besides understanding more by going through this area, it is also usually the biggest single expense area of any business. It is also one that is not often thoroughly audited by the IRS because attention is usually drawn to the more regular or mundane areas of T and E and other benefit type expenses. It is possible to have various personal expenses or capitalizable items buried in the cost of goods sold and written off in the normal course of operations. Although you may find such a situation to be the exception to the rule, it is not that difficult, once familiarity with the business and its books has been obtained, to go through the cost of good sold to determine if what is being posted to that account is proper and reasonable.

7
MAJOR EXPENSE AREAS

"Round numbers are always false."

—Samuel Johnson

EXPENSES IN GENERAL

In general, all expense items, or at least the ones that appear to be significant, can merit an investigation to determine whether there are any personal expenses being run through the business, the appropriateness of the business relationship, and to indicate normal, operational, recurring items. However, various expenses are typically more relevant and/or more likely to be of significance in an investigation. These include payroll, rent, depreciation, and retirement plan contributions. Of course, depending on the business, various other expenses may be of paramount importance.

PERSONAL USE

Many types of businesses offer their officers or owners the ability to utilize the business's products, supplies, or whatever in their personal lives. Our concern is with more than just the customary use of office stationery, pencils, or postage. The value of those items is usually too immaterial to be concerned with and therefore, would only cheapen your work product if included. However, where dealing, for instance, with a retail food store, the personal use of the business products may extend to well over a thousand dollars per person per year. With a family of four or five you could be talking about a few thousand dollars of food each year being consumed personally and expensed through the business. A similar situation might also occur with a clothing manufacturer or retail clothing store. In fact, in each type of business, it's almost something that can be taken for granted, though so called common knowledge or common practice, when accusing someone of using thousands of dollars of company assets personally and not reporting them as income, may be a little difficult to get across in an acceptable fashion. It, therefore, requires additional legwork on your part. For instance, the analysis of the personal financial records should help to determine on what money was and was not spent. Certainly, the absence or near absence of clothing purchases in the personal financial records of someone in a business where clothing is sold, would strongly suggest the personal use of the business's products. There are a plethora of other areas where personal use can amount to significant dollars. Examples of such businesses are department stores, gift shops, drug stores, furniture dealers or manufacturers, and automobile dealers (new or used).

Upon discovering that company assets are being used personally, as described above, the amount must be removed from business expenses, and added to personal disposable income. It should be kept in mind that if you are using the cost of goods sold to back into a sales figure where the sales number is in dispute because of the cash nature of the business, you should, prior to finalizing your calculations, remove from the cost of goods sold the extent of personal use. Failure to do so keeps the cost of goods sold artificially high which, when using percentages for gross profit to back into gross (actual) sales, forces a higher sales figure than is correct, and damages your report.

OFFICER SALARY

Officer salary is a very important area in your investigation. Prepare a schedule of officer salary — whether it be simply a recurring payroll item or whether it fluctuates significantly enough to require a line-by-line analysis. This schedule will have a multitude of purposes: it will enable you to compare the salary to the reported income, trace net salary to personal account deposits, watch for any variances or changes in salary, and compare the salary to the salaries of other companies in similar industries (industry norms). In addition, this schedule will also be part of the overall payroll analysis in terms of total payroll reasonableness in relation to payroll as it pertains to that industry.

Reasonable Compensation

A significant factor in our investigation is called reasonable compensation. This is not the same as the IRS concept of reasonable compensation, although there are underlying similarities. The approach is that any officer salary in excess of a reasonable one is more appropriately deemed a return on capital, and should not be treated as an expense of the business, but rather as an after-tax disbursement to an investor. To the extent that any excess exists, expenses are reduced by such, thereby increasing unreported profits. Of course, if there was a recent IRS tax exam, and if it covered this area, it may prove useful. This is not to say that the IRS' examination in this or any other area is accepted as gospel. However, it does indicate that another outside third party came up with a finding that might buttress your own.

Besides comparing the magnitude of officer salaries to industry norms, there are certain other approaches that may be taken to help support your findings as to whether or not compensation is reasonable. It is one thing for an officer to take an inordinately large salary and then, for you in your report, to credit some of that back to the earnings of the business, thus indicating that the salary is unreasonably high, and represents, in part, a return on investment – a dividend. However, it is another thing if perhaps there are two or three officers – especially if the officers are related and/or if they are all stockholders. Question whether the salaries are justified, not merely reasonable. You may be facing a situation where there are family members, in no-show jobs.

No-Shows

Citing from my experience with a couple of automobile dealerships, in one such case there were a few family members involved in the business, and all were receiving salaries. However, investigation of the W-2's indicated that one family member lived out of the country. Considering that it was an automobile dealership, it was highly unlikely that a salary was actually being earned by that family member. At another dealership, inquiries of personnel indicated that one family member, who was allegedly working in the business, in fact had no function there. Various personnel had indicated that he was never around, and an analysis of the various job functions of the officers indicated that one of them performed virtually everything, and the other performed allegedly only one significant job function. Furthermore, that one job function was actually covered by a rank and file employee. Investigation indicated that the office in which this family member allegedly worked was clearly an unused office. This was determined because of the basic emptiness of that office and its work sterility. It had dust all around, it was totally unused, it had no personal effects, etc. All the evidence pointed to a no-show job with significant compensation, for a relative who was close to the operating family, and who also was a significant stockholder. Again, in identifying no-show jobs, you must keep your eyes and ears open, think about what you are doing, and think about the approaches necessary to properly complete your work.

Salary Reduction Plans

Does the executive's salary fluctuate substantially — that is, not in line with the company's volume or profitability? This is generally not an issue where the person being investigated doesn't have some significant degree of control over his source of salary. In the typical closely-held corporation, it is possible that you might see the owner/shareholder receiving a salary for some years of, for instance, $100,000 and then all of a sudden, in the last year or two before or just subsequent to a divorce action, the salary drops precipitously to perhaps $50,000. And further, that such drop is not reasonable in light of the company's volume and profitability. Such a situation might be indicative of divorce planning. That is, the executive might be intentionally reducing his reported income for reasons relating to his divorce, such as planned desires to diminish the perception of his ability to support his soon-to-be ex-wife. Any fictitious reductions in income should, in some way, be either discounted, disregarded, or adjusted in your report.

Outside Income

There is the possibility, as we have experienced, that there might be compensation to the officer(s) outside of the books of the company, which is perfectly legitimate in operation and treatment. Specifically, as observed in a couple of investigations of law firms, it is not unusual for one or more of the lawyers to receive income directly, in his or her name, from a municipality or a school board, or for a director-ship of a bank. This compensation is even at times given in the form of a W-2, withholding taxes and all, in such a format that the partner/officer is left with no choice but to report this compensation on a personal tax return.   However, as far as the law practice and the partner/officer are concerned, it is widely and uniformly viewed as part of the practice's income.   The general treatment of this is that the gross amount of that compensation is an offset against what that attorney would otherwise be entitled to receive through the practice.

The effect of outside income on the 1040's is rarely a problem because it is reported.   (There is certainly nothing wrong with this nor is there any intimation that there is anything wrong.)   However, it is critical that this outside income be added back to the practice's gross, and that same amount reflected as compensation, so as to properly reflect the magnitude of the gross receipts of the business and the gross compensation of the practitioners.   This is clearly so, not only because the firm recognizes such as an offset against the agreed to compensation package, but also because such work is generally performed on firm time, using firm resources and support, and usually is an extension of the firm's legal work.

Officer's payroll yields much useful information.   A proper an-alysis will aid you in determining its reasonableness, disposition, sources, and whether or not it's justified at all.

PAYROLL — OTHER

Payroll is often the largest single expense line in many businesses. It can be found in virtually any department of a business — whether it be cost of goods sold, selling, administrative, overhead, or dis-tribution.   Though there can be many variations of magnitude, even within an industry, the overall payroll should evidence some degree of reasonableness.   The reasonableness of the payroll, however, may not be easy to determine, especially where a company has a large payroll.   After all, pulling out $20,000 or $50,000 from a five mil-lion dollar payroll may not give you enough of a variance from the norm to mean anything.   An investigation should involve, at the very minimum, going through W-2's (making sure that the totals tie — that you have seen all the W-2's), and looking for familar names and addresses — relatives or friends.

An approach to utilize in analyzing payroll, when you have your suspicions but have made no progress using more conventional approaches, and one that is usable only in limited circumstances, is to obtain the payroll cards or the equivalent time sheets and analyze them. The concept here is that if you suspect there are no-show jobs, but are having a problem feeling confident about your hunch, perhaps an analysis of time cards will reveal certain people who should have time cards (the nature of their jobs is such that they should have time cards if they are legitimate employees) but who, for some reason, don't have them. In most situations, "no-shows" do not fill out time cards. Although a discovery in this area might not by itself be conclusive evidence that the person without a time card is in a no-show job, it may lend support which enables you to pursue your hunch.

Be sure to reconcile the payroll per the W-2's to the general ledger or, if a fiscal year business is involved, do whatever tests are necessary to satisfy yourself that you have all the W-2's for the period(s). This is an area where input from the other spouse, former business associates, or employees can be especially important — that is, they can assist in recognizing paramours, family members with different names, and other people that are especially noteworthy. The idea is to satisfy yourself that the payroll is what is necessary for the business and no more. The treatment of any payroll that is not a proper business expense can take a couple of different forms. It may involve treating it as salary to the principal. Alternatively, it may be deemed that in total it represents more than a reasonable amount of compensation to the officer and, therefore, rather than compensation, is additional company profit.

RENT

Although rent expense, in most situations, is clearcut and simple, it is an area that is also often material and must not be overlooked in your investigation. It is important to ascertain to whom rent is being paid, what the monthly rent is, and where and what the premises are for which the rent is being paid. For instance, are there business locations such as another office or warehouse; or perhaps personal premises, such as someone's apartment; or perhaps monies are being paid directly to an individual for rent expense. Is the rent being paid to an unrelated party, or some related or controlled party, in which case the question of legitimacy of the rent and its arm's length nature becomes an issue. If the rent is being paid to a related party, has the other end (that is, the receipt of the rental income) been accounted for appropriately in whatever books and records exist on the receiving end — and have you accounted for it in your report (if applicable and appropriate).

We have seen, in the course of various investigative assignments, situations where a personal apartment (rarely do we see a home involved in this) is paid for as an expense of a business. It is generally easy to verify such instances. If you've ascertained there is an unrelated party being paid rent at X per month, and if you multiply that by 12, and the result comes out to be the number reflected in the books and records of the company for the year, then you really have no more to do in that area. It is one of the few constant expense areas that you will come across.

Review The Lease

Along with your analysis of the rent expense you must obtain a copy, or at least review a copy, of the lease. Besides the usual need to review a lease during a typical audit, there is also the possibility that you may come across a hidden asset. In many commercial situations, a lease is assignable and, if a long-term lease, may have a value in and of itself. The author had the opportunity to come across a professional service business that had offices in a major metropolitan area with a long-term (twenty-year) lease with approximately five years remaining. The lease was originally written, with an unrelated party, at the going rate (also in this case, there was the situation of a tenant in a strong bargaining position and a landlord hungry for tenants). After a few years of inflation and substantial pickup in the area's rental market, the lease terms were fully $20 per square foot below the going rate. Considering that this office was over 10,000 square feet, it was easy to appreciate how one of the most valuable assets of this practice was its lease. Apart from any tangible assets of the practice and its goodwill, the lease itself had the potential of being sublet at $200,000 per year profit. Of course, the other side to this is that, for the last couple of years, and for the next few years, the business benefited by paying less rent than the going rate, if it were to sublet its premises, the business would have to find a new location, presumably at the current market rate. This of course, made subletting the premises, from an operational point of view, unlikely. Nevertheless, concerned about the value of the business at a point in time, that lease's "hidden value" was a significant factor.

Change In Location

Perhaps you've analyzed the rent and found it to be at arms length and reasonable. There are still a couple of other possibilities. In one situation, a company, during the most recent fiscal year, moved to a new location. For several months, the company paid double rent — for the old premises, which it was still occupying, and for the new premises, which it was preparing for use. This doubling up of the rental expense had a significant depressing effect on the company's profitability for the most recent year. It was also a nonrecurring type of expenditure and, therefore, was disregarded for our purposes. We added back the new office rental (which represented the office that was not being used) as it was not properly indicative of the rent expense of the business for that period of time.

A similar situation that we investigated involved a business which had, during the past year, moved into new and smaller quarters. The business was not doing particularly well — one reason was that its overhead was too high. A major reason for this high overhead was that its premises far exceeded of what was required. Subsequent to the move, the business's operations, style of operation, volume of business, etc., did not change to any appreciable degree. In order to present in a report what the business had actually done and what it could be expected to do in the future, it was necessary to adjust the past rent expense, (legitimate as it was) to reflect the current circumstances of the business, such that a prudent investor/manager would know what to expect from the business in the future.

Again, it should be kept in mind that where we are concerned about the ability of a business to continue to generate income, and where we are presenting financial data to assist a business appraiser in the valuation of a business, the critical question is what will the future realize, not what has been the past experience — even though the best, most reliable measure (in general) of expectations for the future is the past.

Being The Landlord

Although we would not get directly involved in the valuation of rental property (that's the domain of a real estate expert, not an accountant), where a couple has rental property, there may be the question as to how much is currently being rented. It is not unheard of for an individual who owns a multi-unit dwelling, to reflect only some part of the dwelling as being rented, even though all of it is rented. For instance, suppose that an apartment building with 20 units, has 18 units that are reported rented. First, without being sure of exactly how many units there are, we might assume that with 18 rentals there are 18 units. Or, even if we know there are 20 units, perhaps two are vacant. To accurately determine the total number of units requires an investigation of the property in person, input from all interested and informed parties, and a thorough analysis of not only the business, but the personal financial situation of the owner(s) as well.

Depending on the situation, what goes unreported on rentals could be the difference between a break even cash flow and a very profitable one. For example, you might be concerned with a vacation residence at the shore, with a season probably 12 weeks long — even though only 8 weeks are shown as rented during the summer (or if a ski resort, the winter). This discrepancy can involve thousands of dollars of unreported income. Also, just because it is a shore property with summer rentals, doesn't mean that there isn't a winter resident as well — paying a much lower rent, but nevertheless paying rent. This analysis is extremely important for an appreciation of the cash flow of the parties.

DEPRECIATION

Is It Reasonable

As we accountants know, depreciation is an area with extreme latitude, even since ERTA (1981) placed certain restrictions on methods and lives. Hence, the depreciation schedules maintained by a company or by its accountant must be reviewed. What methods of depreciation are being used? Especially if the methods are accelerated, it is likely that the assets are carried below fair market value. Similarly, that would mean that the expenses are overstated vis a vis their true economic costs. What lives are used for these assets? An abnormally short life would indicate a tax maneuver (not very unusual) to accelerate the depreciation as much as possible.

When you come across short lives or accelerated depreciation, a judgment must be made as to whether it is justified and whether book value is understated. If, for example, a Mercedes is being depreciated over three years, it is a safe bet that the car is worth far in excess of its book value. Or, if a building is being depreciated over a 15 year life, it too, most likely, is being depreciated too quickly. Adjustments in this area have the dual effect of reducing expenses by slowing down depreciation and increasing the assets, thereby increasing the book worth of the physical operation.

What assets are being depreciated? They should be reasonable in the context of the business. For example, I came across a small business depreciating a luxury car. Depreciation of several thousands of dollars was being charged to a company that only grossed a $100,000 or so. That business hardly warranted the use of a car — let alone a luxury car.

The reconsideration of proper depreciation, from a financial statement point of view, has taken on added significance since the passage of the Economic Recovery Tax Act of 1981. That Act brought on the now well known Accelerated Cost Recovery System (ACRS) method for depreciation. It is generally recognized that, notwithstanding the use of ACRS for tax purposes, it is not an acceptable method for financial statements. Nevertheless, in many situations where it is felt that there are no material differences, or in various other situations where the finer points of financial versus tax presentations are ignored, you may very well find that you are faced with depreciation schedules based on ACRS. Also, where you need to work with the tax returns, perhaps because there are no financial statements, again, you will be working with ACRS (of course, only as to assets acquired since 1981). In some cases, ACRS may be appropriate or at least reasonable; in other cases the amount of depreciation may not be material enough to warrant any adjustments.

On the other hand, let's look at one of the classic areas of depreciation adjustment — a luxury car. Virtually any car is depreciated below book value under ACRS, inasmuch as 100% of the cost of the car is written off in just three years. (This is obviously prior to the Tax Reform Act of 1984.) This becomes significant when dealing with an expensive car. For example, a $40,000 car, after three years, could be carried at $0 on the books, when it is more likely that that car is worth perhaps $20,000 or $30,000 after three years. In fact, it could even still be worth $40,000. While this particular situation has been somewhat mitigated by the Tax Reform Act of 1984, conceptually these concerns remain. The point is that whereas many other expenses require merely a determination as to whether or not the expense is properly documented and supported as a business expense, depreciation requires a judgmental decision as to the appropriate magnitude of depreciation after you have determined or accepted that the asset is a business asset.

Depreciating Investments

Another factor affecting your analysis of fixed assets is an asset that is not necessary for the proper functioning of the company, such as a building. The question then becomes is the building more of an investment rather than an operating asset, in which case the expenses used for carrying it are not properly chargeable against the business. For example, where a medical practice owns the building in which it is operating, there can be many expenses for that building and, in fact, the expenses may far exceed a reasonable rental. This does not mean that the doctor does not understand what the rental market is, but rather that he or she may view the expenses as an investment in real estate which he or she owns. This factor must be reflected by taking such an unnecessary asset and related expenses, out of the practice's structure when determining its true operating expenses, and inserting in its place, a reasonable rental to be factored in as an expense of the business.

Occasionally, you come across some rather odd depreciation situations. For example, we investigated a business that purchased a significant amount of artwork during the year, to furnish its new offices, and this artwork was capitalized and depreciated. Unless you're dealing with run-of-the-mill, department store artwork (and in this case we weren't — we were dealing with quality artwork, each piece costing over several thousands of dollars), in the long run, there is no economic reality to depreciating art. In fact, there has been litigation over the tax-based inability to determine a reasonable life for a piece of artwork. Without a determinable reasonable life, artwork cannot be depreciated (or an investment tax credit taken). What often is the situation in the case of artwork acquired by a business, is that it is a fringe benefit for the officer or owner and, in many cases, is located in his or her house. Thus it's rather bold to depreciate such artwork as if it was some form of a wasting asset.

RETIREMENT PLANS

Anytime retirement plans are an item in the expense structure of a business, there is another wrinkle — another element of the investigation that must be addressed. (The verification and acceptance of the plan expense is easy.) You need to at least investigate the plan records to determine the magnitude of the last few years' allocation of contributions (and forfeitures) to the person being investigated, and the magnitude of that person's account balance at the end of each of the last few years. You may also have to analyze loans made from the plan to related parties/parties in interest — especially the party being investigated. Also, if the officer/owner uses the retirement plan as a savings vehicle for voluntary contributions, the plan must be viewed as another source of assets and income of the parties involved.

If a retirement plan is a defined benefit retirement plan, it is possible that the plan is underfunded, and thus is a liability to the company, which reduces its net worth. This has a similar depressing effect on the net worth of the individual. It is also possible, although less likely, that the plan could in fact be overfunded (by having excess monies deposited therein), and if the excess funding was deducted in past years (rather than having been established as a prepaid expense on the company books), then you'd have an additional asset — in the form of a prepaid contribution by the company.

Vesting

As all readers are probably aware, retirement plans have provisions for vesting. Vesting, briefly defined, means ownership. That is, 60% vesting in one's account balance in a retirement plan means that whatever your account balance is (or, in a defined benefit plan, whatever the retirement benefits to which you are otherwise entitled), you irrevocably own 60%. If you were to leave today, and your account balance was $10,000, you would receive $6,000 of that $10,000 — forfeiting the other 40% or $4,000.

When doing investigative accounting work, if the party being investigated is a principal in the business, it is unlikely that the principal's account balance in the retirement plan can be accepted at anything less than 100% vested — regardless of the formalities of the number of years in the plan and the actual percent vested. The reason for this is that except in a situation where the party being investigated has a minority interest in the business (and even then the practicalities of being a substantial owner of a business are such that one rarely, if ever, loses a nonvested interest), from a practical point of view, the officer/owner never forfeits anything — being able to force termination or amendment that would result in 100% vesting. Arguments to the contrary are without foundation. For instance, we have seen arrangements whereby a departing doctor received additional compensation from the remaining doctors, above and beyond what their agreement called for, because of the nonvested portion of his retirement plan that he was supposed to forfeit. They all agreed that they would treat it as if it was 100% vested, even though the money had to be left in the plan.

At this point, you have read about the investigatory process for the major P and L items — sales, cost of sales, payroll, rent, depreciation, and retirement plans. In general, if there are major wrongdoings to discover and/or major adjustments warranted, you would have discovered them by this stage. There still remains much to do — numerous expense categories to analyze. The next chapter covers many of the accounts yet to be reviewed. Your findings for most of these accounts will be far easier to document, objectively and conclusively, than were your sales or payroll findings.

8
OTHER EXPENSE AREAS

"I never travel without my diary."

—Oscar Wilde

This chapter covers the many other operational expenses common to most businesses. Many of these expenses come to mind when the concept of executive perquisites (for instance, travel and entertainment, repairs and maintenance, miscellaneous and office expenses) is broached. Depending on the magnitude of the abuses, these areas can yield relatively little or quite a substantial treasure trove of ill-gotten fringes. Either way, as long as there are some personal/nonsupportable expenses paid by the business, the ability to detail them in your report is important and will increase your leverage during negotiations.

To analyze personal/nonsupportable expenses select certain months that seem to warrant investigation; analyze the specific disbursements that make up those months' expenses; vouch both the cancelled checks for propriety of endorsement and payee, and the documentation supporting those expenses. Keep in mind that a cancelled check is merely proof of payment, it is not proof of the purpose of the payment or of the legitimacy of an expense. If an invoice cannot be found, perhaps the expense was not legitimate. Unless you are satisfied that invoices are missing because of sloppy internal control rather than a deliberate attempt to obfuscate the issue (especially if a recurring event), it is likely that information is intentionally being kept from you.

When investigating the bills associated with these personal/nonsupportable expenses, look for such things as the nature of the product purchased. For example, if an office supply bill was for a snowblower, and you know that the company has no need for a snowblower because it is a tenant and the owner assumes the responsibility for snow removal, it is likely that it was purchased for the personal use of one of the officers.

You must remember to look for the address to whom the bill is directed. It is a fairly good bet that unless there is a strong correlation in identification between the person and the business, if an invoice has a personal residence address on it, the bill is of a personal nature. However, this is not always the case for if there is a strong personal tie between the business and the individual, it is not unusual for vendors to ignore the formalities of a business structure and put down whatever address they are used to carrying. On the other hand. even if it is the business address that appears, it is not unusual for an understanding to exist between the supplier and the company such that the bills will be addressed to the company, their actual use or delivery site nowithstanding. There is no easy rule of thumb in this area – it is something for which you have to get a feel and an understanding.

REPAIRS AND MAINTENANCE

Repairs and maintenance expenses often include items associated with personal (for instance, home) maintenance or, where legitimately business expenses are possibly capitalizable rather than expensable items. It is not unusual to see major repair items expensed, rather than capitalized – for tax purposes. Furthermore, even if the items are for business and even if legitimately expensed, if they are unusual and nonrecurring they should be removed from your financial presentation – not because of their legitimacy, but because of their relevance for the future.

Perhaps there's a lawn or cleaning service being paid through the business. An immediate question to raise is, Is any of this personal in nature? Is it the residence lawn that is being maintained, the business lawn, or both? This is sometimes very hard to determine – unless the lawn service is accommodating enough to give accurate and honest detail on the billing. Of course, if the business doesn't have a lawn, your job has been vastly simplified. You cannot always rely on vendor billing detail inasmuch as most vendors will accommodate a good customer by giving a business address on a billing rather than a personal address.

We have seen personal lawn care, garage door openers, painting, general maintenance and repairs, carpentry and plumbing, and many other types of home maintenance expenses run through businesses.

Sometimes the personal nature of such expenses is relatively easy to discover — such as when the residential address is indicated. Other times, however, it is not nearly as easy and it may even be necessary (notwithstanding one party or the other's intimate knowledge of the facts) to subpoena the vendor. Regardless of whether business or personal, unless there is a burning desire or need to present the investigated party in the worst light, the consequences of subpoenaing third parties or doing exhaustive analysis in this area is justifiable only when the numbers involved are substantial. You do not go through all this effort just to prove that the $250 painting of a child's bedroom was expensed through the business.

INSURANCE

Whether you analyze the insurance expense account or the prepaid insurance account or, more typically, both, the intent is the same and generally three pronged — What assets are covered? Are any personal expenses being paid? Is the prepaid expense correctly stated?

What Is Covered

You must make sure that you understand the extent of the coverage of various items. For instance, we came across a situation where the coverage for the inventory was 50% (well over $400,000 extra) above what was shown on the books. As we suspected, the insurance account was a giveaway that the business was carrying, and that there was considerably more inventory than was being shown. The other side of the coin is that the business was reporting less income than it actually realized. This was not, by the way, a situation of LIFO, but rather the more mundane inventory cushion.

Especially where the available funds are relatively tight and perhaps your client is not willing to pay for a real estate appraiser, at least some indication of the extent of insurance coverage for a building and its contents will give insight into what the property *might* be worth. This does not, in any way, substitute for a professional real estate appraisal, but in a pinch, for negotiation purposes at least, might be useful.

Another example of how an insurance analysis will lead you to understand more of what is in a business and what its assets are, involves a trucking business. We found it very difficult, because of poor cooperation, to obtain sufficient information from which to ascertain the extent of the physical assets of the trucking company — the truck cabs and bodies. To circumvent this problem, we reviewed the insurance bills, and from these, made a schedule of all the vehicles and bodies covered. This proved most useful. In fact, there were several pages, giving a reasonable amount of detail and specifics as to just what was being insured. The schedule also gave us information as to the serial numbers of the cabs, and the approximate original cost of each of the items insured.

Personal Expenses

A second approach used for insurance analysis is to verify that only business expenses are being paid through that account. It is not unusual to find personal insurance expenses paid through a business — homeowner, boat, automobile, liability, life, hospitalization, etc. The last two expenses, hospitalization and life insurance, are just as often classified as insurance expenses as they are employee benefits.

Prepaid Expense

A third concern and use of insurance expense analysis is a simpler one. Is there an adequate provision for prepaid expense? Most of the time, insurance policies do not neatly fit a company's fiscal year. That is, there is an overlap between years and typically the premiums are paid up front. This creates prepaid insurance. Although a business on an accrual system will, most of the time, reasonably account for prepaid insurance, a cash business will often write off insurance as paid, with no recognition for the prepaid amount. This is usually fairly easy to determine and to calculate, and is often not significant because if it has been applied consistently, recalculating the current year's insurance expense (reducing it and deferring some to the next year), requires similar recalculation for the previous year and the year before that, etc. The ultimate result, except where insurance has been escalating rapidly or where the business has been expanding rapidly, is that there is no material change in expense from year to year. However, as to an asset at the end of the time period of your investigation, the recognition of the existence of prepaid insurance is a factor, though not usually a material one.

TRAVEL AND ENTERTAINMENT

Perhaps the classic expense category for investigation and for the realization of personal expenses being paid through a business, is travel and entertainment. It is also known as promotion, business development, entertainment, or even advertising. Whatever its nomenclature, this area is one that under most circumstances deserves an absolute beeline for your attention. Common in this area is the use of charge cards — typically American Express, Diners, Carte Blanche, MasterCard, or Visa.

It is imperative when analyzing this expense to obtain the hard copy original receipt — not merely the monthly billing recap. Much information is missing if that backup is not available. For instance, most credit card accounts will give listings of the names of the stores, restaurants, hotels, or whatever in which the money was spent, the date, and the amount of expenditure. However, what they don't give you is some of the information on the hard copy. For instance, the signature of the person who signed for it; or detailed breakdowns such as a hotel bill which included a purchase at the gift shop. It is not uncommon to find that a spouse or a child has signed on a number of charge slips — an indication (especially when it's a child) of the likely personal nature of the expenditure.

In assessing the nature of travel and entertainment expenses, detail, whether in the form of the summary given by the charge company or the individual charge slips, will help (when put onto a schedule by day and type of expenditure) to give you an idea of the extent that one personally benefited from a business. Notwithstanding the possibility that various entertainment expenses would withstand IRS scrutiny, and notwithstanding that these expenses might very well be legitimate business expenses, if your analysis shows that the party being investigated virtually lives off of the business — one or two meals a day, four, five, or six times a week for example — then, from an economic point of view, that person is receiving substantial unrecognized income from the business. While this compensation may not be taxable, it is economic income and, to a degree, should be added back in your computation of the compensation level of that individual. An employee earning $60,000 who has the normal living expenses for a family, is not in the same financial situation as a corporate officer earning $60,000 who has all of his or her lunches and dinners paid through the business.

AUTOMOBILE EXPENSES

Like travel and entertainment expenses, auto expenses deserve detailed attention. We frequently see charge cards (of the various oil companies) with the charge slips indicating the use of several different family cars by several different people. This would indicate that the spouse and the kids are getting in on the act, and that the business is paying substantial personal expenses. Also not unusual, are charge slips for gas at locations well outside of the business area. For instance, we have seen where the executive's son or daughter was allowed to use a company credit card while away at college. We noticed repeated gas usage in a state over a thousand miles away from the business being investigated. These were often on the same day that there was gas being signed for by the executive in her home state.

Charge slips sometimes give such information as license plate numbers. These too may be very useful and prove the existence of multiple cars, the support of other people (i.e., a paramour), the use of personal vehicles, etc. On one occasion, when questioned, an executive explained that the wife's signature was on the credit card because while the officer was busy doing his job, she took the car and filled it up with gas. Similar reasons have been given for children's signatures on cards. Even when the license plate number is not on the charge slip, or even when it is (apparently) the business or executive's car, this argument rarely is credible.

TELEPHONE

A test check of telephone bills should help you to decide whether there are personal bills being paid through the company. One likely sign is if there are two checks each month made out to the telephone company, although this is not always an indication of personal expenses, inasmuch as there might be two different telephone systems, two different numbers, or some other justifiable reason for having two payments. Nevertheless, two payments warrant investigation. Even one payment warrants an investigation because, as you might guess, the telephone company will accept checks from anyone. It doesn't matter that the check may have to be split among two or three telephone numbers.

Your test check of telephone bills can be correlated with your investigation of the personal bank accounts. If you determine that there were no telephone bills paid personally, it strongly indicates that unless you have come across that rare individual without a house telephone, the personal telephone bill is being paid through the business. Although it is not usually warranted because of immateriality, an analysis of business telephone bills might disclose a large number of expensive, personal calls, perhaps made at unusual hours or weekends, or to distant areas where the business had no reason to call. This would indicate heavy personal use of the company phone. However, unless extreme, the personal use of a business phone is not an item of special note.

There may even be times when a rather unusual twist to the analysis of the telephone expense may prove to be fruitful. Rather than the customary checking of the expense to verify that it is the business phones and not the personal phones that are being paid for, it may prove useful, though only rarely, to do a detailed analysis of perhaps a few months of telephone bills — both personal and business — not as to the expense, but rather as to the specific calls. That is, you would analyze the toll calls on the monthly bills; note the city and state, the area code and telephone number, the time of day of the call, and the length of the call. You would do this where you see unusual calls or what appear to be unusual in terms of length of time or location and frequency, or where you see the same number being called several times. Most of the time, this will be a waste of time. However, where perhaps you have reason to suspect that there is something to be discovered, but you haven't been able yet to put your finger on it, this analysis may just give you some guidance or lead the way to a discovery of import. Once you have those numbers, they aren't useful unless you can find out to whom they belong. This can usually be done through the telephone company — whether it be through straightforward questioning or some surreptitious approach. Certainly, check with your client for whatever input he or she may have.

PROFESSIONAL FEES

Professional fees is one of the few areas for which I generally insist on a 100% analysis. Except for businesses heavily into litigation (product suits, patent infringements), or those subject to petty bureaucratic regulations, analyzing the professional fee expense area is usually an easy task, compared to the detail involved in many other expense account analyses. In general, such analysis can be, pound for pound/posting for posting, the most fruitful area of your investigation. The professional fee area has larger ticket items and more important postings than most expense categories.

Why a 100% analysis when test checking is usually sufficient? With professional fees, it's often not the fee that's of interest, but rather the import of the services rendered that caused that fee. A bill for $2,500 for representation in union negotiations is not as significant as a bill for $500 for a conference relating to a patent, merger negotiations, a buy-sell agreement, or the liquidation or sale of a plant or division. Invoices for professional (legal, accounting, some types of consulting, engineering, etc.) services can indicate situations of major and lasting importance to the company, even if the invoices are small in amount. After all, some things don't take much professional time, and even those that do, often start out with modest fees.

PAYROLL TAXES

Where you discover that there are no-show jobs, such as a child or spouse on the payroll, depending on the magnitude of the operations of the business, it might be desirable to add back to the profits the duplicated/excess payroll taxes generated and paid by the business because of the no-show jobs. That is, if that money was either paid to the officer or not paid at all but retained as profits, there would have been no additional payroll taxes (presuming the officer is over the FICA limitations). Because of payments to other people, there is duplication of a payroll tax expense. This item, depending on the magnitude of the no-show payroll, can easily amount to a couple of thousand dollars per person.

When you are dealing with a business which, after reasonable compensation, etc., has a bottom line of several hundred thousand dollars or more, adding back a couple of thousand dollars of payroll taxes is not too consequential. However, where perhaps you have a company earning (bottom line after compensation) only several thousand dollars, adding back that extra two thousand dollars or so of payroll taxes may be a significant item. Either way, it is a proper approach — the business should not be burdened with payroll taxes for no-show jobs.

TAX EXPENSES

An interesting area to investigate, which at times will yield surprising information, is tax expense. I'm not simply referring to FICA taxes and other payroll taxes, but nonpayroll tax items that might lead you to the existence of things not otherwise evident. For example, in the course of an investigation in which we were involved, it was discovered in our review of the personal financial records that there was an income tax paid to California — even though the parties involved lived and worked in New York. The actual result was nothing of any consequence, but it suggested the likelihood of assets, income, or some other business connection with California.

It's possible you might come across real estate taxes that could be for the personal benefit of the people involved or perhaps indicate the existence of real estate that isn't carried on the corporate books. The investigation of the supporting documentation for those real estate expenses will help you to obtain evidence as to the exact nature, location, block and lot, etc., of any real estate. This in turn, will help for a subsequent valuation by a real estate expert and will also help you in terms of being able to trace the origin and acquisition of that property and determine how it was obtained — whether through the normal channels of business or through asset disposition and acquisition.

OFFICERS' LIFE INSURANCE

First, officers' life insurance may suggest the existence of or lead the way to the discovery of a buy-sell agreement or some other contractual obligation that requires or makes desirable insurance funding. This can be of great significance where valuation of the business is a concern, whether or not you will be doing the valuation. (That is not to say that any such buy-sell agreement, if it does exist, is the final determinant of the value of the business — but rather that the discovery of such is another element to take into account in determining a value for that business.) Second, it raises the question as to whether such expense is necessary for the operation of the business, or whether it is a fringe benefit that is of personal use to the executive and unnecessary from an operational point of view. Third, it suggests the possibility, unless it is only term insurance, of an asset — cash surrender value — that may not be reflected on the company's books.

EMPLOYEE BENEFITS

Employee benefits are often called medical plans or medical benefits, fringe benefit accounts, medical coverage expenses, or whatever. It is typical in most businesses to have at least one expense category for medical related expenses. In closely held businesses, it is very common that there are medical expenses for the officer and his or her family included in such an expense category. We analyze this area to determine to what extent it is represented by more or less standard type of medical insurance which, for most purposes, is a normal operational expense. While it would be considered economic compensation to the officer, it would not, under most circumstances, be added back to operations. On the other hand, direct medical expenses (rather than insurance) paid through the business can be substantial, especially when the family is covered and there are several members in the family and one or more are ill. This is clearly additional economic compensation to the officer, regardless of the tax legitimacy of the medical reimbursement plan, if any in fact exists. Again, our concern is not the niceties of the tax law, but the economic realities of the compensation package to the officer/owner.

It is also interesting to keep in mind that where there are substantial medical expenses (outside of the insurance coverage) being paid through the business, it is presumable that the business should also recognize, on occasion, a negative medical expense in the form of medical insurance reimbursement. This would be so unless the expenses submitted to the business on behalf of the principal are reflected net of reimbursement received directly. Except in that circumstance, the business, by virtue of "suffering" for the medical expenses, should also benefit from the medical reimbursement due on the insurance policy. In the absence of such, it would appear likely that the officer is benefitting twice — first by having the business pay the expenses, and second, by getting the reimbursement from the insurance company personally.

The medical expense category also often includes disability policies and other such fringes. Usually, only the top peple benefit — this is an area not generally offered to the rank and file in most closely held businesses. Many times pharmacy bills are paid through the business and classified as medical expenses. Under most circumstances, this is certainly a legitimate type of medical expense for the business to pay for (ignoring any fine tax points at this time) and, of course, economic compensation to the individual. However, when vouching a sampling of invoices from pharmacies, we have had the occasion to come across situations where the bills included nonprescription type items — clocks, chocolate candies, and various sundries that are commonly sold by pharmacies.

INTEREST FINES AND PENALTIES

Other than when interest is in the form of innocuous bank service charges, it should be investigated to determine just what obligations are being paid for by the business. Verify that these are business obligations and not personal obligations; that there was a business need for this rather than merely a way to generate an expense that was perhaps done to worsen the company's financial position (this is unlikely); determine the disposition and use of the funds generated by the assumption of the liability.

Although fines and penalties, for the most part, are nondeductible, it has been our experience that most businesses deduct them anyway. It is also our experience that they are generally operational expenses regardless of their tax deductibility and, therefore, should not be added back to income. Or if not deducted, should be allowed as a financial presentation deduction against income to reflect the practicalities and realities of the business world. Penalties and fines are a fact of life in many areas and, inasmuch as we are interested in the economic approach and not the tax approach to income and other factors, we must be even-handed and reflect that a legitimate business expense is such regardless of its tax deductibility. However, we have seen situations where there were some rather substantial and unusual penalties and fines that were expensed through the business. Although our investigation indicated they were legitimate and proper as far as their business nexus, and from an operational point of view were expenses, those fines and penalties were extraordinary and not to be considered as recurring expenses. Therefore, they were to be discounted as to the expense structure of the business. What was involved in one case was some degree of incompetence by the business's employees, and oversights by management that allowed these penalties to happen. It was unlikely that such would happen again and further unlikely that, considering what the true income capabilities of that business were, those expenses should be permitted. Of course, we are talking here of unusual, extraordinary, and substantial penalties − not a few hundred dollars because of improper payroll tax fillings.

BAD DEBTS

One of the only reasons to review the bad debt expense account is to see if it suggests to you the writing off of what should be perfectly good receivables. This could happen where payment on these receivables is made, in part or in whole, directly to the officer/business owner; or, where older but still good receivables are written off as uncollectible, a list maintained "on the side", and the receivables then "forgotten" and collected in due course by the officer/owner. If this is happening, it's additional income/compensation, and likely of substantial magnitude.

The bad debt expense account is also reviewed, as would any other account, to determine if it includes an unusually large item that would have to be considered nonrecurring and, therefore, added back to income. Contrarily, if the year was unusually good, with bad debts much lower than several other years, it might be necessary to adjust that year's bad debts to reflect the normal/average level that should be anticipated.

OTHER EXPENSES

Along with miscellaneous expenses, the *office supplies* expense category is often used as a dumping ground for a multitude of odds and ends that don't seem to fit anywhere else. For the most part, there is usually little to discover in this account − unless it has been abused. What will show up in a reasonably thorough analysis is whether any equipment − i.e., a computer, a copier, a telephone system − that should have been capitalized was instead expensed; or, if a substantial amount of personal expenses were paid in the guise of business expenses.

Office supplies, as most other expense categories, can be prescreened with an eye towards large and unusual items; and, like most other areas of our work, has the potential for abuse from several directions — cash checks, personal expenses, and items that should have been capitalized.

The area of *membership and organization dues* and related *subscriptions* is usually not very fruitful in an investigation, except in two areas. You will at times find that organization conventions and related types of expenses get posted to this account. A simple cursory analysis of the account should quickly give you answers to whether that prospect is likely — if there are no large amounts then it is unlikely that this account has been burdened with such types of expenses. This can give you entree into the relevant trade organizations and potential sources for information and comparables for that line of business. Again, keep in mind that the work that we do is on one level, an information gathering tool. Certainly we have to understand that information, collate it, and present it properly. But we must have the raw data — the information with which to begin. Knowing the trade organizations to which this business belongs is one facet of being able to gather the information and put it into a coherent and relevant report.

The concept behind analyzing *utilities* is very similar to that regarding telephone expense. However, while every business and every person is expected to have a telephone bill, not every business or every person is expected to have an electric, a gas, or an oil bill. Thus, if you were to see that a company pays oil bills, yet the company is in an office building where it doesn't have the responsibility of directly paying utilities, it's probably paying personal oil bills. Or, if the company has its own building and it is fueled by gas, why would it be paying oil bills? You must understand what the company does, how it operates, and even its utility bills to determine the extent of any personal use in this area. Again, an investigation of the personal checking account that reveals no such utility expense, would strongly suggest that the company is picking up that tab. Also, usually there is a service address on the utility bill that might differ from the billing address. This too may highlight the personal nature of a particular bill.

MISCELLANEOUS EXPENSES

Any time there are items of substance posted to the miscellaneous account, we must make a point to review it. For instance, if upon going down the miscellaneous expenses category in a general ledger that's posted monthly, we find that there's never more than $100 or $200 posted thereto in any month, then we would not bother to analyze the account.   Any such analysis would likely be a waste of time.   This is not to say that there isn't anything there worth looking at, but rather that you have to make an intelligent guess as to the allocation of your time (and client's money).   Also, as with any expense category, or other category, if you do a reasonable test check of the books and records (just as you would for an audit), you should be fairly confident of discovering any pattern or substantial amounts of wrongdoing, misclassifications, or personal expenses paid through the business.   It does not guarantee that you will discover everything — only that, within a reasonable range and within a justifiable economic cost structure, you will likely uncover whatever is worth uncovering.

As a general rule, our concern is with recurring items — things that establish a pattern.   It is likely that wherever any such pattern does exist, or where a substantial item is worth investigating, any intelligently developed work program or attack format will bring out such an item.   It's not unusual, in the miscellaneous expense category, to find, by the very virtue of its being "miscellaneous," that there are just one or two months with significant postings, with the rest of the months being immaterial.   In this case, as with any other expense, you would zero in on those months.   It's hard to say in advance what you might expect to find in a miscellaneous expense account, but it can be almost anything, including mispostings, or having the account operating as a suspense account until somebody makes a decision to reclassify.

9
PERSONAL FINANCIAL ANALYSIS

"Cursed war and racking tax have left us scarcely raiment to our backs."
−Sir Walter Scott

There will be times when you have done all of your investigative work, and you have come up with little or nothing in the way of additional income. You haven't been able to find the hidden source of cash income, excessive personal expenses being run through the business, or anything else that really enables you to establish with certainity, (and with the ability to testify on the stand) the fact that there is more income than what is being reported. Certainly, this might mean that everything is aboveboard. If you still have your doubts, there are other techniques to use to determine the validity of the reported income. Some of these are regularly used by the IRS in its fraud investigations and when used properly, have a track record of success in withstanding cross examination.

Change In Net Worth

Trace the changes in net worth from a period of time to another period in time − i.e., from three years before the filing of the complaint to the time of the complaint. This requires getting a starting point of all assets and liabilities − developing a personal balance sheet. It might facilitate the gathering and comparison of figures if year end dates are utilized, rather than attempting to restrict oneself to the complaint date. Use of such an approach should not adversely effect the validity of the results. Keep in mind that changes in value are not the issue − only income and outlays. Increases or decreases in market value that have not been realized by the actual sale or liquidation of assets are of no consequence in this test.

It is imperative to know the reported income and expenses for those years. Reported income is usually not too difficult to determine in that you can refer to tax returns, using gross income with reduction for income taxes withheld, less payments due with the tax return of the previous year, and add previous year tax refunds, inheritance or gifts, noncash items such as depreciation, or the sales proceeds (rather than gain/loss) of security transactions, etc.

The expenses may not be as easy inasmuch as many of them never show up on tax returns because of their personal/nontax related nature. For that you need to go into the checking and savings accounts of the individuals and, depending on the extent of the accuracy of the records involved, you may have to make certain assumptions. Interview the parties involved and reconstruct their standard of living, making some educated guesses as to what they spent on such mundane expenses as food, clothing, and various other elements of living that often leave little or no residual financial trail. Be as thorough as possible inasmuch as you are on less stable ground (even though the ultimate result may be a very supportable one) than if you had come up with proof in the form of actual cash deposits that were not reconcilable to reported income.

Once you have calculated the various components of this net worth test (more accurately − changes in net worth) you are in a position to put the pieces together. The beginning of the period net worth plus the income and loan proceeds, less the expenses and loan repayments, plus or minus any adjustments should equal the end of the period net worth (without reflection of purely market value changes). It is almost a certain bet that if anything is truly remiss, you will have significant unaccounted for differences. However, even if you have done your work properly, and your reconstruction suggests that the income is as reported, there is still room for substantial error − in the form of unknown assets − i.e., a hidden cash hoard in some vault, jewelry, or gold or fine metals stashed away. Without some concrete proof there is little that can be done against careful and meticulous deception.

Standard Of Living

Perhaps you don't have enough information to do a net worth test, or perhaps the net worth hasn't changed significantly, but there is still strong reason to believe that there is hidden income. Then perhaps a standard of living analysis would bear fruit. Part of your work involves getting a feel for the couple's (in a matrimonial suit investigation) lifestyle and standard of living. That feel, in conjunction with your review of various financial records, will in some cases tell you whether your feeling is in sync with the information on the financial record. For example, if the couple lives a very high lifestyle, with expensive clothing, vacations, and frequent dinners out, and yet the financial information available to you indicates a rather modest income level, there are implications of cash income and/or the business paying personal expenses. Contrarily, if your review of the personal financial records indicates a rather modest lifestyle, yet the known income sources are substantial, there is the possibility of asset retention and, therefore, expectations of a substantial net worth. It is important that the lifestyles, the business income, and what you have observed all make sense in the context of the overall picture. Of course, you must be careful not to overlook the possibility of a living style generated by going into debt. That is, do the individuals maintain a luxurious living style by virtue of continually increasing debt, and not by using their own money.

Personal Financial Statement

It is standard practice to ask for a recent personal financial statement from the parties concerned when you are doing an investigation, in order to make the necessary comparisons and contrasts between the business and personal records and financial conditions, and also to make comparisons between the way net worth has increased (or decreased), and contrast it to the reported net income of the parties. However, frequently you will be advised that either there are no personal financial statements, or you may be given a current financial statement that was prepared for the specific purpose of addressing the divorce investigation. You really want the personal financial statement that was prepared a year or two ago — before the initiation of the litigation and before there was a perceived need to denigrate one's financial position because of the potential for litigation. Where do you get these financial statements? Look for indications of loan activity. It is common that for any substantial loan, whether business or personal, a personal financial statement is required, which is on file with the bank and should be obtainable — by subpoena, if necessary. For a business loan, when dealing with a closely held business, especially one that is not very substantial and/or has not established a long track record with the lending institution, a personal financial statement is an absolute requirement. Such may be required for the annual renewal of a bank credit line, or for perhaps equipment financing for the recent acquisition of new fixed assets or real estate such as a home mortgage. The point is you must keep your eyes open for the likely sources from which to obtain a personal financial statement — which may be very candid rather than one prepared in anticipation of litigation. It should be recognized that at times people have a tendency (especially where finances are borderline or where personal businesses and egos are involved) to inflate various items on personal financial statements. Be watchful for such puffery.

When preparing a personal financial statement, do not forget to include a tax refund receivable or a tax balance due. It is easy to overlook these items in that with a personal, unlike a business financial statement, you do not have a set of books that gives easy access to such information. It is therefore important that you reflect the extent of a tax refund expected — computing it pro rata — proportionately for the portion of the year represented by the "as of" date on the financial statement. On the other side, you also must take into account a pro rata approximation of what the tax balance due will be — allowing for the extent of withholding and/or estimated taxes paid through and including the "as of" date of your report.

Collections

Some people maintain a part or even most of their wealth in the form of collections of tangible assets. These collections can be coins, stamps, bottle caps, baseball cards, paper clips, cow chips, comic books, guns, beer cans, antiques, or whatever. You might be able to discover the value of such by analysis of disbursements or insurance policies. The existence of a collection should be known (in a matrimonial case) by your client — spouse — unless the person being investigated is so secretive that he or she has managed to hide such a collection. Collections represent another area with the potential for hidden and/or undervalued assets and, if substantial, warrant the engagement of a qualified appraiser to determine value.

1040 Analysis

Personal tax returns can be a wealth of information. For example, in one case in which the author was involved, the tax returns indicated thousands of dollars of contributions. The support (prepared by the individual on a sheet of paper without substantiation) listed various charitable organizations with contributions ranging from some small amounts to over a thousand dollars each. Our thorough analysis of the personal checking accounts indicated no such contributions. This raised three possibilities, one of which (the concept of the contributions being in cash) was discounted immediately as impractical and illogical, considering the level of financial sophistication of the individuals, their lifestyle, and the magnitude and the frequency of the contributions. The other two possibilities were that either there was another checking account not revealed to us (denied at that time), or that the contributions listed on the return were false, grossly overstating the actual contributions. If such was the case (which it appeared to be), it helped to cast doubts as to the credibility of the party being investigated, which helped to improve our credibility, and strengthen our report and bargaining hand.

In another case, there were some serious questions raised as to the magnitude of income and the standard of living. The tax returns, on Schedule A, indicated very substantial (thousands of dollars a year) sales tax deductions. The explanation and support for such deductions was that there were heavy expenses for items subject to sales tax. Support in any form, other than as prepared by the taxpayer, was nonexistent. We utilized the sales tax figure to simply back into the gross amount of expenditures that would have had to have been made to generate the magnitude of sales tax deductions reflected on the tax returns. This, along with various other facets of the personal life style of the individuals, indicated that either there was significant unreported income (similar to the concept previously described regarding contributions), or the deductions for sales tax on the returns were fraudulent. Although we couldn't be positive either way (and we couldn't substantiate either point), one of those two points had to be the case. In either case, our position was strengthened, and the position of the investigated party was weakened.

There are many other areas where a review of the tax returns can reveal information that perhaps wasn't known (to you) previously, or that at least helps to further explain things. These areas include the Schedule D — security transactions, which can help to explain various cash flow items; the Schedule E, which gives information regarding investments and partnerships, trusts, and S corporations that may prove useful in discovering information or investments of which you previously had no knowledge; the itemized deductions, where perhaps there are union dues that might suggest the existence of a heretofore unknown pension.

Schedule B may list several different banks. This will tell you that you have at least those accounts for which you will need copies and which you will need to investigate. Your analysis of Schedule A may indicate real estate tax deductions far in excess of what should be there, based on known information. This may suggest other real estate owned, and for which deductions are being taken. Or, perhaps there might be a casualty loss for a collection. The existence of a collection itself can represent a significant hidden asset. Furthermore, the casualty loss deduction may include an indication of a substantial insurance recovery — a cash flow item of relevance.

It is a good idea to also review the state tax returns, especially if you suspect that municipal bonds may exist. Even though such bonds would not be reflected on the federal return, they might be reflected on the state return to the extent that they are not exempt by the subject state.

In this chapter we have seen how various personal financial matters have a bearing on, and are an integral part of our investigatory work, and how some of these directly relate to the analyses of a business. We have seen that changes in net worth, standard of living, personal financial statements, collections, and tax return analysis are of great importance, especially when dealing with a cash business.

10
THE FINAL STAGES

"An expert is one who knows more and more about less and less."
—Nicholas Butler

REPORT AND NEGOTIATION

Your report should be in a logical sequence, self-explanatory, and include a narrative (even if in note form) of what you observed, problems you had (if worthy of note and if additive to the report — not merely griping), and anything else that would help to flesh out the substance of the report. For example, you might include a paragraph highlighting that you were not allowed to inspect all the records you requested, and, therefore, your ability to render a complete and/or satisfactory report was impaired. Or, you might indicate that there were contradictory statements made and contradictory information supplied to you. Consequently, certain areas of the report might be incomplete. It is desirable to include a page or two of background information to give the reader an introduction to and an understanding of the company that you investigated. This also serves to show that you had an understanding of the business, which is crucial to your credibility.

Virtually any adjustment to the reported income or balance sheet should be explained either in a narrative or, more preferably, in a note form that can be readily traced and tied to your report. For example, if you were to add back $5,000 of travel and entertainment, you should have a note explaining in some reasonable detail your basis for such an action.

Reports can take many different forms, and must be adapted to the specific circumstances. For example, you might be engaged simply to determine the correct income of a business. I had such an engagement. I was called in because, as per the agreement at the time of divorce (which had occurred two years prior to my engagement), the records were to be opened up for alimony redetermination. Thus, it became solely a matter of determining the correct present income of the medical practice. You may also be called upon to illustrate the tax consequences to both parties, of various levels of alimony vs. support, perhaps with several assumptions as to other income sources.

One of the functions of your report is to help to arrive at a settlement; that is, to help the parties avoid having to go to court and having a settlement thrust on them. Of course, litigating is more expensive for the parties, more timeconsuming, less sure as to outcome, and usually less satisfactory than a settlement reached out of court. Your report can play a crucial role in that settlement by showing the parties that you have done your work, that you have thoroughly analyzed the situation, and that you have come up with a factually based report that neither side can seriously contradict. Or, if there is room for reasonable subjective judgment, at least your report is persuasive enough that both sides, especially the one you are not representing, agree that it would be prudent to arrive at a compromise settlement. If you can accomplish that, you've accomplished your purpose, perhaps even more than if you had gone to court and testified. None of this is to say that if you have to go to court (if the parties can't settle) your report is deficient or at fault in any way. There are many times when no one, short of a judge with an ax, is going to get the parties to settle.

As it is common in settlement negotiations to involve an investigative CPA, you must be very well prepared, at least as well as if you were going to court. Your role must be that of the professional, although in negotiations, you can at least be somewhat of an advocate. You should go into that settlement well versed about your report, supporting workpapers, data, and also about the tax ramifications of the likely settlement options. Your role in the settlement negotiations must be clearly defined between you and the attorney, well in advance of any such meetings. Unless given the green light by the attorney, your role in these negotiations is always subordinate to his or hers. After all, the attorney is the advocate and the one who's responsible for putting together the right settlement. You are the expert — the independent, unbiased accounting expert whose role in negotiations should involve assistance, information, explanation, and technical advice, and not argumentation and advocacy.

THE EXPERT WITNESS IN COURT

To be effective as an expert witness in court, a number of areas require your attention. You should know the difference between giving an opinion as an expert witness as opposed to giving an opinion in an audit situation. You should be able to prepare exhibits (including charts and schedules, as and if necessary) that are, in addition to factual, easily understandable to nonaccountants. You must be able to objectively analyze other experts' reports, and succinctly point out to the attorney with whom you are working, the strengths and weaknesses of those reports. It is important in advance to be aware of, and prepared to make, the necessary commitment of time to serve as an expert witness in court. You must be able to be precise, succinct, and understand that the techniques for being an expert witness are somewhat different than the traditional auditing and accounting procedures and techniques. The fact that virtually all of your work product is discoverable should caution you as to the content of any side or parenthetical notes on your worksheets.

Your services will help to develop and strengthen a court case by freeing the attorney involved from accounting and financial matters, so that he or she can focus on law. The information you provide will put the attorney in control of the facts and thus enable the lawyer to present his or her case as effectively as possible. The information you provide, and your general input will assist in developing questions to be asked and obtaining additional information from your adversaries. An informed, savvy financial/tax expert — you, the accountant — with which to discuss ideas and approaches, and from which to glean insight, is a valuable tool to an attorney.

Don't Advocate

You obviously must be objective. Do not present yourself as an advocate — that would ruin your value as an expert witness, and endanger your reputation. As far as your reputation, keep in mind that in most states, or at least in general regional localities within those states, the divorce/chancery courts become a community of practitioners who get to know each other fairly well (including the judges), and who trade information about mutual reputations back and forth. If you become no better than a hired gun, a whore, that reputation will stay with you for quite a long time, and damage your ability to function as an expert witness — to say nothing of the devastation it could wreak on your ability to retain valued referrers.

It is certainly desirable, for a number of reasons, that your fees be paid in advance of your testifying as an expert. Not the least of these reasons is the fact that we all like to get paid as soon as possible. However, when testifying as an expert witness, having your fees paid in advance (at least for services rendered up to the time of testifying) will help to avoid any appearance of a fee contingency situation. From a practical point of view, however, especially when representing the spouse that's on the "outs" in a divorce case (typically the wife without an independent source of income), it is virtually impossible, where you've developed substantial fees (a normal situation when it involves a business investigation of any substance), to collect your fee in advance. Moreover, such situations are rarely, if ever, viewed in a negative light inasmuch as the practicality of these cases is widely recognized.

Be Prepared

As professionals, we're all cognizant of the need to prepare in advance for a conference with a client; you don't go into a conference to discuss financial data without having first reviewed them. This is more important and more essential when you're going either for depositions or, especially, for a court appearance. With a client, you won't normally get the third degree — your relationship typically is such that you'll be asked questions of a routine or anticipated nature, which you probably can handle either factually or extemporaneously, based on your experience with the client. If a question involves something that appeared to be a mistake on the financial statement, or involves something for which you don't have a good answer, normally there's a certain grace allowed by your client, and you can always correct the statement. Besides, having done a good job and having scored a lot of points in the past, you're not perfect, and we can understand some minor errors. However, this is not the case when you're in court. You're not dealing with a friend. You are going to be given the third degree — most of us are not used to that. You can expect to be asked some very difficult and pointed questions that will require straight factual answers — not assumptions based on your experience over a long period of time, which you just don't have in this case.

You must be sure that you're familiar with the work product produced by your subordinates — not just your own work product. Your work files must be well-organized, so that you don't spend an unreasonable amount of time flipping through them to arrive at the necessary papers to support your report or your statements on the stand. Not only do you want to avoid spending a lot of time going through your files, but if the records are readily and easily available, you will enhance your professional image in the eyes of the court, your client and attorney, and your worthy opponents. In court, you cannot afford to be embarrassed or put on the spot with something with which you are not familiar, because you'll not easily get another chance to correct or verify your statements nor will any ineptitude be overlooked as minor. The more you, and subsequently your report, can be damaged/impugned in court, the stronger the other side's position is.

The Truth

Although it shouldn't be necessary to state this, honesty and straightforward answers are essential in court. The slightest indication that you're being less than candid — that there's some taint to your testimony — will torpedo your credibility and your ability to continue and be considered an expert witness. There's been more than one professional whose reputation has been irreparably tarnished by not being prepared, by hedging on an answer to the extent that doubt can be cast his way, and even worse, by compromising his integrity through a slanted report, or by covering up a failing in his or her fieldwork.

Keep in mind that besides one's own self-esteem and sense of responsibility and accomplishment, no client or group of clients is worth compromising your professionalism, damaging your reputation, potentially risking the loss of future references in this field, or getting the reputation of a hired gun and, in the extreme cases of malfeasance and incompetence, losing your certificate. This type of work has enough obstacles in it, enough risk and potential for antagonism on all sides, and (especially where you don't discover the hidden pot at the end of the rainbow) dissatisfaction even from your own client, that adding to that slew of problems by doing anything less than a professional and quality job is simply inexcusable.

11
TAXES AND DIVORCE

"Being asked whether it was better to marry or not, he replied, 'Which-ever you do, you will repent it'."

—Diogenes Laertius

INTRODUCTION

Though this is a book on investigative accounting, it is reasonable to include a chapter on aiding the parties (the reference here is obvious-ly to matrimonial cases) as to cash flow and tax consequences. In fact, there are many who feel that this is merely another facet of our work. That is, our natural orientation towards a tax background puts us in the position to evaluate (and suggest) various alimony alter-natives and the resulting cash flow and tax consequences. The reader should keep in mind that this chapter in no way attempts to be an authoritative dicta on the tax ramifications of divorce. It is merely a useful overview.

It is common, especially when representing the stereotypic wife in a matrimonial case, that you'll be asked to prepare a budget for your client. Or, perhaps you'll be asked to utilize an already pre-pared budget to determine the amount of before tax income (typically alimony, sometimes a combination of alimony and wages and/or interest/dividend income) necessary to generate, after taxes, funds sufficient enough to maintain a targeted standard of living – the budget. It's important in these cases to take into account all taxes. That is, don't overlook the FICA tax on wages, and don't overlook state income taxes. Another possibility, not typical with our more routine tax planning procedures, is that in divorce cases, a spouse may move to a different state. In such a situation, your budget, tax analysis, and planning should allow for the taxes in the state in which the spouse whom you're representing is expected to be. Also, if representing the wife, you will often utilize head of household rather than single rates. Obviously, this presupposes that there will be a dependent child (whether or not the exemption of the spouse whom you're representing) living with that spouse.

TAX PLANNING AND ALIMONY

It is common to be asked to project two or three alternatives as to combinations of alimony, outside earnings, interest and dividends, etc. For instance, the amount of the alimony may very well be contingent upon the magnitude of an initial up front cash distribution, from which the spouse will receive interest or dividend income. The more interest or dividend income, the less the need for alimony.

We had an interesting situation not too long ago, involving a stereotypic high income earning husband and a low income earning wife. Because of the husband's numerous tax shelters, however, his income bracket was actually lower than the wife's. Therefore, our recommendation to the parties involved was to significantly reduce the alimony that the husband would otherwise pay to the wife, and instead, pay a substantial amount of child support. In this particular case, to maintain her middle income lifestyle and that of the three children who were to live with her, she needed, in addition to her earnings, approximately $42,000 of alimony. While the husband could afford it, taxwise he did not need such a deduction. We illustraded to both parties how they would both be better off if the $42,000 alimony were restructured to be $15,000 of alimony and $15,000 of child support. The wife would come out ahead by over one thousand dollars after taxes, and the husband, because of his tax sheltering, would not only save an initial cash flow outlay of $12,000 per year, but would actually, after taxes, despite the nondeductibility of the $15,000 of child support, save over one thousand dollars. Consideration and much thought had to be given to the concerns of potential remarriage and maturation of the dependent children. Nevertheless, it was evident that both parties would benefit by treating a portion of the payments as child support. What this highlights is that when as investigative and tax accountants we represent proposals, we should be aware of possible alternatives that would benefit the parties, even if these alternatives are atypical.

We best serve our client when we best balance our client's financial and economic needs with the practicalities and realities of what the other side can afford. In the preceding case, our effort to help our client obtain the magnitude of support necessary to maintain her lifestyle became much more palatable to the other side when it was structured in a way that reduced the gross amount. Obviously, when doing such work, we are representing our client, and not the client's spouse or business adversary. However, an inflexible or prohibitively expensive position, regardless of how emotionally or theoretically justified, will not sell, and will further alienate the parties involved. The result could be protracted and expensive litigation, rather than a rapid and amicable settlement.

TAX PLANNING IN GENERAL

One of the more interesting areas of tax concern in investigative services, mainly when dealing in matrimonial cases in which you represent the wife, is planning for the new tax status that the wife (and this also applies to the husband) can be expecting. Both spouses, who previously filed jointly, are now faced with filing either single status or head of household status returns. If the arrangements in the interim are not structured properly, it could result in the catastrophe known as married filing separately. Keep in mind (as the author has seen this overlooked by other practitioners many times) that in the typical situation where the wife retains custody of the children but the husband has them as exemptions, being able to utilize the head of household status does not require being entitled to the dependency exemption. If the children live with the wife, she is entitled to head of household status — notwithstanding her husband's exemption deduction(s).

The CPA can be called in to assist an attorney and a client purely for tax purposes. This may be to augment the investigative services, but need not be — it can simply be to help with tax problems — the most typical tax consultant type of situation which, for the most part, is outside the scope of this text. You will often be dealing with a client whose tax knowledge is virtually nil, and with an attorney whose tax knowledge can range from nil to far superior to yours. We have come across many situations where competent attorneys, who have sound tax backgrounds, also recognize the advantage of having an outsider for assistance, such as a CPA well-versed in taxation. If for no other reason, this assistance is important in that it provides tax alternatives from an independent expert rather than from an advocate attorney.

The role of taxes can become unusually critical depending on what's involved. For example, in a divorce action on the West Coast, one of the assets available for distribution was a block of stock that had originally cost $500,000 and was, at the time of settlement, worth $100,000. The husband had agreed to transfer that block of stock to the wife — valued, of course, at $100,000 for that element of the property settlement. The husband did in fact transfer the stock to the wife based on the attorney's advice, but did so approximately one week *prior* to the divorce. When the husband attempted to write off the $400,000 capital loss on his personal tax return he found, much to his distress (and subsequently much to his attorney's distress), that the IRS has a very strong position regarding a transfer between spouses; namely, such a transfer does not create a tax deductible loss. The IRS deemed this to be a transfer between spouses, notwithstanding their obvious adverse interests, and disallowed the $400,000 loss to the husband. To make matters worse, the wife benefitted by receiving a $500,000 cost basis for this $100,000 asset. If the husband's attorney had more tax savvy, or had utilized the services of a tax oriented CPA, that same transaction would have happened *after the divorce.* The two would no longer have been related parties, and the IRS would have had no problem with the transfer — and the husband would have had the tax benefit of the $400,000 loss. This was a pre-TRA 1984 situation: tax law has since been changed.

TAX REFORM ACT OF 1984

The Tax Reform Act of 1984 included major changes in the tax aspects of domestic relations. For instance, some of the changes in the property transfer area were long overdue and meritorious reforms. Still, other changes in the alimony area have the potential to cause disaster and havoc, which strongly suggests that various provisions were not well thought out.

Transfers Of Property

A major change brought about by the Tax Reform Act of 1984 involved the treatment of transfers incident to a divorce; this is commonly known as equitable distribution. The main thrust is that the Davis case was overturned and its tax impact altered, such that all property transfers subject to the Tax Reform Act of 1984 are considered nontax events. What this means is that no gain or loss will be recognized, or that no depreciation or investment tax credit will be recaptured upon the transfer of property between spouses — even incident to a divorce. Such transfers will henceforth be considered gifts and not a sale or exchange of property. Thus a recipient spouse (transferee) gets a carry over basis, and the donating spouse (transferrer) relieves himself or herself of the property without any tax impact.

To be incident to a divorce, the transfer must either be within one year after the marriage terminates, or must be interpreted as being "related to the cessation of the marriage." The nonrecognition rules apply if a transfer is made up to six years after the divorce. However, the burden of proof is upon the transferee such that he or she must show that the transfer was incident to the cessation of the marriage. After that six year period, there remains a rebuttable presumption that the transfer was not related to the termination of the marriage. Holding period, basis, and all other attributes of the original ownership (whether that original ownership was in joint or in individual name) get transferred to the new owner. This nontax situation even applies if there is a transfer of an asset with liabilities in excess of basis. These rules apply to any post July 18, 1984 divorce agreement where the transfer is also after July 18, 1984. If the transfer occurs after July 18, 1984 but the divorce instrument is executed prior to this date, or conversely, if the transfer is before July 18, 1984 but the instrument is executed after this date, the new rules will apply if *both* parties so elect.

Tax Impact

It is important to note that merely because such transfers are now nontax events, this does not mean that taxes do not play a role in property split-ups upon a divorce. Taxes remain as important as ever — it is just that their impact, for the most part, has been swung to the transferee (recipient) instead of transferrer, and have been deferred. To illustrate the shifting of the tax burden, with the recipient of the appreciated property inheriting a latent gain, observe the following:

ASSET	FAIR MARKET VALUE	BASIS	LATENT GAIN	LATENT TAX	NET EQUITY
A	100	100	0	0	100
B	80	20	60	12	68
C	20	10	10	2	18
D	0	-100	100	20	-20

Note that in the above situation, if one spouse were to keep asset A, and the other spouse were to keep assets B, C, and D, even though each spouse would receive $100,000 of fair market value, the spouse with A would get $100,000 of real equity; whereas the spouse with B, C, and D would obtain only $66,000 of real equity (68 + 18 – 20).

There are other potentially serious tax ramifications associated with this shifting of the tax burden. For example, if a husband in business transfers a business asset on which investment tax credit was taken to the wife, and the wife is not in business, upon receipt by the wife of such property, it ceases to be Section 38 (investment tax credit) property. The wife, as transferee, would have the potential investment tax credit recapture liability. Some surprising zingers could come about from this rather unusual circumstance.

Another interesting point to keep in mind is that if a transferrer is a dealer in real estate, for instance, a transfer of such real estate to a nondealer transferee (a spouse) will not cause that property to be inventory in the hands of the transferee — the transferee can treat such property as an investment and therefore be eligible for capital gain instead of ordinary income treatment. It should be further noted that the transfer of accounts receivable or an installment sale obligation are also eligible for the general nonrecognition rules; such transfers will not trigger income realization. Finally, it should be noted that the transferrer has the obligation to supply the transferee with all pertinent documents in support of basis and other tax attributes. It appears that if such obligation is not met, the property's treatment at the time of transfer is subject to the old Davis rules.

Alimony

The second major area involved in the Tax Reform Act is the treatment of alimony. The new law has eliminated concerns involving "support" and "periodic" and has, to a degree, simplified the concerns as to whether or not a pay out arrangement will be treated as alimony or as a property settlement. Several specific requirements must be met in order for payments to be considered as alimony and thereby deductible by the payor and taxable to the payee; and certain options remain. These are as follows:

1. Payments must be in money as opposed to property.
2. The payments can be to the former spouse or for the benefit of the former spouse. The instrument can provide for payments to third parties with the consent of the former spouse.
3. In the agreement, the parties can specifically provide that even though payments to be made under the agreement contain all the indicia of deductible alimony, the payments are not to be construed as alimony. This is an almost unique situation where the parties can disregard otherwise effective tax rules and designate the tax treatment of payments.
4. Payments, as under the old law, must be made as per a divorce decree or separate instrument. A decree or written instrument or a separation agreement or Pendente Lite order will qualify.
5. If the parties are legally separated but not yet divorced, alimony cannot be deductible unless the parties are not members of the same household. Therefore, where spouses live under the same roof, even though separately, payments between them are not considered alimony.
6. The divorce agreement must state that there is no liability to make payments after the death of the recipient spouse, nor can the agreement provide for substitute payments to the estate. Even though such payments do commonly stop upon the death of the recipient spouse, the agreement must explicitly state this; if not, the payments are not considered alimony.
7. Attempts to disguise child support in the form of alimony will probably no longer work. If payments are to be reduced in accordance with a contingency relating to a child, the payments to that extent will be construed as child support. For example, if the payments of "alimony" get reduced at the date a child turns 21, graduates college, or some other event

within the child's life, the amount of modification will be considered as child support and thereby not deductible/taxable.

8. The alimony terms may provide, although they need not, for termination of the alimony upon the death of the payor or the remarriage of the payee.

Front Loading And Recapture

Perhaps the most disturbing element of the new alimony rules is the new six year rule. Payments must be required in each of the six consecutive calendar years starting with the first year in which alimony is paid. Pendente lite payments, since temporary, are excluded — they don't count towards the six year test. However, payments under a separation agreement, if they are pursuant to a consent decree, will qualify.

The basic rule here is that the first $10,000 each year presents no problems. If there are payments in excess of $10,000, however, some very tricky tax planning and tax considerations may come into play. This largely came about from a misguided attempt by the Internal Revenue Service and Congress to counter some perceived front loading abuses.

The new law provides that payments in excess of $10,000 in any one year are not to be considered alimony unless such payments are made in each of the six post separation years. Years for which no payment is made (because of the death of the husband or wife, or remarriage of either spouse) do not violate the six year rule, even if they bring it up short. Any year in which these alimony payments are in excess of $10,000 less than they were in a prior year, there is the potential for recapture. This recapture income situation can be devastating. For example, assume that an agreement calls for a wife to pay her husband $4,000 a month in alimony for six years. So far so good. For the first three years the payments are dutifully made. In year number four, the former wife suffers severe financial reverses and makes no payments. In year number five, the dutiful ex-spouse has a good year and makes up the payments that she missed in year four — making payments of $96,000 in that year. In year six, the regular $48,000 is paid.

The above situation results in the following: in years one through three, $48,000 is deductible by the wife and taxable to the husband.

In year number four, the wife has no deduction – but she has recapture income of $114,000. This is calculated by subtracting the $10,000 floor from the $48,000 paid in each of the previous three years, resulting in a $38,000 excess over the zero that was paid in year four – resulting in three years of $38,000 per year recaptured, or $114,000, in year four. The former husband in that year gets a $114,000 deduction – whether or not his tax return could use such a deduction and, therefore, whether or not it really amounts to any tax benefit to him. In year number five, the wife gets a $96,000 deduction for paying same and the husband picks it up as income. In year number six, when payments revert to the normal $48,000, the ex-wife has recapture income of $38,000 – the $96,000 paid in year five minus the $48,000 paid in year six minus the $10,000 allowance. In that year six, the ex-husband therefore gets a $38,000 deduction.

The way the law currently reads (pending hopefully a technical corrections act or some other move by the powers that be), it does not matter whether the reason for a reduction in alimony is hardship, judicial modification to an agreement, plain orneriness, or no reason at all. The exception to this fluctuation nightmare is where the alimony is tied to the income of the payor in the form of a percentage of such income. In such a situation, fluctuations from year to year will not present a problem.

These rules concerning alimony are effective for payments under instruments executed after 1984. As to pre 1985 instruments, if they are modified after 1984, the new rules will come into effect.

Other Aspects Of TRA – '84

Another significant change in the domestic relations area pertains to the taking of the exemption for the children of the marriage on the divorced parents' tax returns. To simplify a much litigated situation, the rules now become very simple. Under the new law the custodial parent gets the exemption. This of course assumes that between the custodial and noncustodial parent they provide more than 50% of the support of the child. If this is the case, the exemption very simply goes to the custodial parent, *unless* both spouses agree to a different treatment; namely, that the noncustodial parent will get the exemption. This agreement can be for a single year, for varying (even nonconsecutive) years, or forever. It is totally at the discretion of both parties. However, such decision must be made in writing, and such writing must be attached to the tax return of the non-custodial parent for each year that an exemption is taken for such child. Notwithstanding a parent's ability to take the exemption for a child, medical expenses paid on behalf of that child will qualify as deductible medical expenses, with the normal 5% threshold necessary.

There are other changes brought about by the new law and by a subsequent law passed later in 1984, the Retirement Equity Act of 1984. The areas affected by these laws include provisions for the innocent spouse, the treatment of alimony trusts, the treatment of transfers of interest in retirement plans and various other areas. These are areas best covered in a tax treatise — not in this book.

OLD LAW — PRIOR TO TRA '84

Even though the Tax Reform Act of 1984 (TRA '84) made major changes in tax planning for divorce, there are many (millions) existing situations unaffected by TRA '84 since, for the most part, it had no retroactive impact. Therefore, I have included the following — old law — to point out still existing situations.

Perhaps the most frequently recurring problem pertaining to taxes and divorce revolves around the issue of deductible/taxable alimony vs. nondeductible/nontaxable child support vs. maybe taxable property distribution. If an agreement is structured (and there must be a written agreement — under almost any circumstances an oral agreement is not sufficient), by labelling payments as alimony or un-allocated support, the intent is obvious, and thus the tax interpretation will be (except in rare cases) such that the payor gets a deduction for those payments, and the payee picks up same as taxable income.

Problems frequently occur when the language isn't explicit or when people do not understand the finer niceties and illogicalness of the tax laws. A prime example of how the situation can get muddled and how the poorly construed tax laws can wreak havoc on the parties involved, is a situation where the agreement reads that the husband will pay for the support of the wife and the two children. Further, that the husband shall pay $1,000 a month in unallocated support for the wife, and that as each child reaches maturity, the monthly payment shall be reduced by $200 — so that after both

PRE-TRA '84

children are out of the house, the wife will be receiving $600 a month. The obvious intent, from an economic point of view, is that the husband is paying the wife $600 for her support and $200 for the support of each child. However, the document doesn't read that — nowhere does it state that the $200 a month is child support. It only states that as each child reaches maturity, the overall support shall be reduced by $200. This beautiful example of tax nonsense has caused much tax litigation — the $1,000 a month is considered plainly and simply unallocated alimony. Therefore, it is fully taxable to the wife, and fully deductible by the husband. The point is, if some portion is intended to be child support (nondeductible/nontaxable), then it must be stated as such in the agreement.

Alimony

What does it take to make alimony and separate maintenance payments deductible? These payments must fall into one of three classifications:

- Payments under a decree of divorce or of separate maintenance or under a written instrument incident to divorce or separation.
- Payments made under a written separation agreement.
- Payments made under a decree of support.

Whether a court order, or some form of written agreement, qualifies under any of the above (other than the obvious final decree of divorce, which clearly qualifies), often revolves around individual state law. This is another wrinkle in the federal tax laws in that it is largely contingent upon what the states consider to be an enforceable obligation.

It is interesting that only those payments made after a divorce, or after a separation agreement goes into effect, are deductible by one and taxable to the other. We have seen many cases where, for whatever personal reasons, the husband and wife separate and yet, while the husband is paying support payments to the wife (and this may go on for several months or several years), there is no agreement other than an oral understanding. The result is that the husband gets no deduction for his payments, and the wife is not taxable thereon. It's

PRE-TRA '84

certainly not the best tax method of handling these payments, though there are likely other factors that entered into the picture.

Periodic

One of the great wrinkles in the alimony issue is that to be deductible, payments must be "periodic payments." It is generally recognized that payments qualify as periodic if they are made either in a fixed amount for an indefinite period, or if an indefinite amount for a fixed or indefinite period. To illustrate:

EXAMPLE 1:   A divorce agreement has the husband paying the wife 30% of his monthly income (which may or may not vary from month to month). The payments are to be made monthly, and are to last for a period of seven years. These payments are periodic — deductible/taxable. They qualify as such since they are clearly payments made of an indefinite amount for a fixed period of time.

EXAMPLE 2:   Very common, is an arrangement in a divorce whereby the husband pays the wife fixed, monthly payments of, for instance, $1,000 for as long as she shall live or until she re-marries. These payments are periodic and deductible/taxable — that is, they are clearly payments of a fixed amount being paid over an indefinite period of time.

Ten Year Test

As with anything tax related that starts out simple, there's no way things are going to stay simple. For instance, consider the situation where instead of some form of open-ended payment obligation, a fixed or a principal sum is to be paid over a period of time. Code Section 71(c) states that for a payment of a principal sum to qualify as a periodic payment, and therefore, deductible, the installments of the principal sum must be made over a period of more than ten years after the date of the divorce agreement or the equivalent. Further, it also states that the deduction in any one taxable year is limited to 10% of the principal sum. To illustrate:

PRE-TRA '84

EXAMPLE 3: A divorce agreement obligates a wife to pay to her husband $230,000 over a period of 20 years. The payments are to be $25,000 a year for the first two years, and $10,000 a year thereafter for the next 18 years — for a total of $230,000. For the first two years, only $23,000 (10% maximum of the $230,000 total) is deductible by the wife and taxable to the husband. For the following 18 years, the full amount then paid — $10,000 — is deductible/taxable. None of the first two year nondeductible amounts may be carried over to a following year and then deducted.

EXAMPLE 4: The divorce agreement provides that the wife shall pay to the husband the sum of $100,000 in eight annual installments of $12,500 each. None of the $100,000 is deductible by the wife or taxable to the husband — the payments are for a principal sum, but over fewer than ten years and, therefore, do not qualify as periodic payments.

An exception to all this, as there are always exceptions in the tax law, is that when these installment payments are subject to a change or discontinuance upon death, change in economic status, or remarriage, they are then considered periodic payments, not payments of a principal sum and, therefore, deductible in full whether or not the payment schedule is for a period of more than ten years. To illustrate:

EXAMPLE 5: The divorce agreement provides that the husband will pay to the wife a total sum of $50,000 at the rate of $10,000 a year for five years. However, the agreement provides that the payments will stop if the wife dies or remarries. As a consequence, even though there is a principal sum stated, and the payments are for fewer than ten years, they are deductible in full by the husband and taxable in full to the wife, because there is a contingency that would cause the payments to stop prematurely.

Is It Alimony Or Property Settlement?

Now let's consider the problems that inevitably occur when taxpayers try to balance their need to arrange their financial affairs for economic purposes on one hand, and tax purposes on the other. For example, the author was recently involved in a situation where the

PRE-TRA '84

divorce agreement provided for so-called periodic payments to be made over a 12-year period (clearly more than ten years, and possibly intended to qualify as periodic because of the greater than ten year time frame) — and that's where the trouble started. The agreement indicated that a principal sum was to be paid, on a monthly basis over 12 years, with interest on the unpaid balance, and secured by property owned by the husband. Notwithstanding the in excess of ten year payout, this type of an arrangement is really a property settlement and, therefore, nondeductible by the payor and nontaxable to the payee. The factors that result in these payments being treated as a property settlement include:

- The payments were fixed in amount and not subject to contingencies such as death or remarriage.
- The payments, together with other property awarded to the recipient, constituted approximately half of all the property to be distributed.
- The payments were secured.
- The recipient's need was not considered in determining the amount of the payments.
- The intentions of the parties in their agreement — not clear in this case.
- The recipient had surrendered valuable property rights in exchange for the payments.
- Unpaid portions would be paid to the recipient's estate.
- The payments were not related in any way to the income of either party.

As there are numerous cases that can be found in accordance with the above, our office, representing the recipient spouse (wife), upon doing her tax return, took the position that only the interest on the unpaid balance of the agreement was taxable to her. While writing this book, both the husband and the wife were under audit. The only open item of the audit was the differing tax treatment on the payments taken by the husband's accountant and the wife's accountant (us). All these problems and expenses would have been avoided if the agreement had been more explicit. Our position turned out to be the prevailing one.

PRE-TRA '84

Exemptions

Another major area of dispute and tax complication is the issue of support and entitlement to the exemption deduction for the children. Just because the divorce agreement reads that, for instance, the husband is entitled to the exemption deduction, doesn't make that statement inviolate of the tax law. The IRS has ways of putting itself in the middle of marital situations. The general rule for the exemption deduction is that the parent having custody of the child for the longer period of time during the year is entitled to the dependency deduction. This rule, though, applies only if the combined support furnished by the parents amounts to more than one-half of the total support of the child for the year and, furthermore, only if the child is in the custody of either or both of the parents for more than half the year. Now that's fine as a general rule. However, the parent not having custody, or having custody for the shorter period during the year, is entitled to the dependency deduction if that parent either contributes at least $600 towards the child's support and the divorce agreement (or separate maintenance or whatever agreement) provides that he/she is to receive the deduction; or, alternatively, that parent provides $1,200 or more of support for the child, and the parent having custody for the longer period does not clearly establish that he/she provided a greater amount of support. The complexity of these rules only adds to the confusion, aggravation, and litigation.

Property Settlement

Another problem area involves the tax ramifications of a property settlement. In a community property state, this usually is not a problem inasmuch as spouses, as a general rule, split 50-50 and, in a community property state, this is considered merely a nontaxable, equal division of jointly-held property. However, in numerous states that are noncommunity property, when one spouse transfers property, which has appreciated in value, to another in exchange for the recipient's "marital rights," a taxable event occurs and the person giving up the property realizes a taxable gain thereon. The gain is the difference between the appreciated value and the transferrer's basis in the property. This is true regardless of whether it is

PRE-TRA '84

done as part of a settlement without benefit of a court order or under a court order. In one of the simplest forms, a joint residence is deeded to the wife in exchange for her marital rights. To the extent of one-half of that appreciation (since it was jointly owned and, therefore, the wife had half ownership prior to the transfer), the husband recognizes a taxable gain. This is, in large part, the essence of U.S. vs. Davis, the landmark case in this area.

There are tremendous inequities in the property settlement area. Just as a simple point, assuming that there are no assets other than a jointly-held residence, there seems to be something terribly unfair and inequitable about one spouse giving up the joint marital residence and, as a consequence, having a potentially taxable event. It's only potentially a taxable event because if the normal two-year rollover provision for the gain on a personal residence is exercised by the replacement in that time period with another personal residence, there is no taxable gain to be recognized. However, in many divorce cases, perhaps in the typical case of the husband giving up the joint residence, and not having custody of children, the husband may move into an apartment. There is then no rollover of any gain. The result stereotypically is that the husband gives up half of the joint residence, has a taxable gain, and gets no cash to pay for the taxes on his fictitious gain. Obviously, this is one of many areas of the tax law that was long overdue for an equitable change.

Revenue Ruling 81–292

The recent issuance of Revenue Ruling 81–292 caused a minor stir in the tax community because of what appeared to be the potential for an easing of the IRS' position (though this is a matter for judicial determination, rather than IRS regulation). This ruling is potentially of great significance in the division of property in divorce settlements — specifically in noncommunity property states. The ruling states that "...an approximately equal division of the total value of jointly-owned property under a divorce settlement agreement in a non-community property state is a non-taxable division. The basis and holding period of each asset is the same as when the property was jointly owned." The specific situation for which this ruling was issued was a property settlement agreement in a divorce that provided for transferring certain joint assets to one spouse and certain joint

PRE-TRA '84

assets to the other spouse. The ruling indicated that if there was an approximately equal division of the total value of the jointly-owned property, it would qualify as a nontaxable division.

Of course, many questions arise from this ruling. For example, just how exactly equal need a division be? Also, it is unclear as to the extent of the state law impact on how far the IRS will be willing to go in applying the definition of jointly owned property. As far as how equal a property division need be, most likely this will be determined by litigation.

Joint Ownership

Perhaps the really interesting question is how far the concept of jointly owned property in noncommunity property states can be extended. It is certainly a matter of fairly complex legal determination and, to a degree, tax interpretation, as to whether or not divorce laws in such states as, for instance, New Jersey, New York, and Pennsylvania are such that, regardless of the paper title of an asset obtained during marriage, in fact, it is jointly-owned property by virtue of the marriage. Under such logic, virtually any and all marital assets might be considered jointly owned. If so, there might be no adverse tax consequences from any split of marital assets that resembles an approximately equal division.

In Davis vs. U.S. (1962), the Court rejected the taxpayer's contention that the transfer of shares of stock constituted a nontaxable division of property between co-owners by stating that "...the inchoate rights granted a wife in her husband's property by the *Delaware Law* (emphasis ours) do not even remotely reach the dignity of co-ownership." The Court went on to acknowledge that had the parties been co-owners of the stock, the transfer would have been a mere division of property and not a taxable event. Do the laws of such states as New Jersey, New York, and Pennsylvania grant a wife (or husband) rights to the other's property that resemble or have the "dignity" of co-ownership?

An interesting possibility in using and applying Revenue Ruling 81-292, is that in anticipation of a divorce situation, it may be wise to mortgage a piece or pieces of property. This could generate cash from which you can manipulate assets by the application of that cash to either a jointly-held account or a nonjointly-held account.

PRE-TRA '84

You may thus create an overall situation that enables you to more easily facilitate the approximately equal division of jointly-held property.   The point is that with some foresight and intelligent manipulation, it may be possible to create a situation that neatly fits into Revenue Ruling 81-292, and thereby avoid all tax problems.

12
CONTRIBUTING AUTHOR CHAPTERS

INTRODUCTION

The work that we investigative accountants do, would not go any-where — would leave a void — without the assistance of at least two other professionals — attorneys and business appraisers. Certainly, by the very nature of the litigation work, attorneys are essential in every case that calls for an investigative accountant. Indeed, I have not had a single such case, without at least two attorneys also in-volved. In addition, while the major thrust of this book involves investigative work in the matrimonial sphere, there are considerable such services rendered to the insurance industry.

Regarding business appraisers, although there are no clearly de-fined requirements to qualify or to entitle one to hold him or her-self as a business appraiser, there are certainly those who are very competent in this area. One guideline for experience and compet-ence are the ASA (American Society of Appraisers) credentials that the professionals have earned. These appraisers have been trained in areas of economics and finance far better than we accountants have. Where a professional (doctor or attorney) practice is being investigated and evaluated, it is very likely that an experienced in-vestigative accountant would be qualified to do not only the investi-gation but also the appraisal. Similarly, an investigative accountant would be a qualified appraiser for certain other types of cash busi-nesses, especially where the accountant has had previous experience.

However, where there is a company of substantial magnitude, a business of substantial complexities, it is essential to engage a busi-ness appraiser in addition to the investigative accountant. The ap-praiser will more thoroughly understand the economic forces that determine the value of the business — once the appraiser has finan-cial figures supplied by the accountant upon which he or she can rely. Also, by virtue of this better understanding, the report will be more complete and defensible and, together with your investigative report, present a much more formidable package. Certainly, there are few things as embarrassing as having to go to court or to conference with attorneys and other interested parties, to defend or explain a report and methodology where you have overextended yourself — especially where you're to be going up against somebody who is not over-extended.

The author is aware of some CPAs' concerns over the additional cost factor involved in having an appraiser in addition to a CPA. Also, some CPA's (a minority) are concerned about the loss or reduction in their own fees. These attitudes are nearsighted and unrealistic. Where there is substantial money involved and the case warrants, the additional expense must be accepted as a necessity. Furthermore, it generally is not a significant additional expense — presuming that someone else, typically in this self-protecting situation, the accountant, would be doing the appraisal and, therefore, the expense would exist under any circumstances. Regarding the loss of fees, there will be a far greater loss of fees if you overextend yourself and get your ears pinned back in the presence of others, especially business referrers. The loss of business from one embarrassing situation will far exceed any fees that you might think you have lost by bringing in another professional. Finally, there is sufficient work of this nature to go around, thus keeping competent investigative CPA's busy as well as competent business appraisers. In fact, the two are allies in this type of work — as I have found, much to my pleasure, with Mr. Jay Fishman, a leading appraiser, whose offices are in Narberth, Pennsylvania.

The following chapters detail what the investigative accountant should expect in terms of demands upon his or her skills, by the legal profession and by the insurance industry. The author was most fortunate to have two very prominent, competent, and skilled practitioners to author these chapters.

WHAT AN ATTORNEY EXPECTS
AND NEEDS FROM
THE INVESTIGATIVE ACCOUNTANT

GARY N. SKOLOFF, ESQ.

In a divorce case, perhaps the most significant decision made by the attorney in preparation of the case is the utilization of an investigative account who will do the following:

A.   Provide a meaningful net worth statement as of the date the divorce action was commenced.

B.   Compute the amount of each spouse's annual salary and other taxable income (i.e., fringe benefits and perquisites of employment).

C.   Provide analysis of the tax consequences of the payment of alimony, child support, equitable distribution, and counsel fees for each party.

D.   Assist the business appraiser in valuing the business interest maintained by a spouse.

Once an attorney and a client have reached the decision that an accountant's services are necessary, a meeting between the client and the accountant should be scheduled to discuss the details of the case. A financial history of the marriage should be taken by the accountant, with the attorney and client present. The accountant should discuss the terms of his engagement with the client and follow that up with an engagement letter setting forth the fee arrangement.

It goes without saying that the attorney expects the accountant to be cooperative, and prepared to exercise reasonable professional care in performing his investigative services. Where warranted, the accountant may find himself assisting in the settlement negotiations between the attorneys, their clients, and the opposing accountants.

Usually, the accountant is expected to review the books and financial records of the commercial entity in question, and submit a report based upon an examination of the aforementioned documents. Additional sources of information include a review of

A.   Answers to inquires from his client.

B.   Answers to interrogatories.
C.   Books of account and related financial records, including savings accounts and checking accounts.
D.   Answers to depositions.
E.   Individual, partnership, and corporate income tax returns.

In a substantial case, the attorney expects the investigative accountant to examine the personal transactions of the litigants involved. That investigation should include examination of the following:

A.   Copies of individual federal income tax returns.
B.   Bank statements and cancelled checks.
C.   Photostatic copies of all savings account passbooks.
D.   Copies of stock transactions and brokerage account statements.
E.   Copies of any financial statements submitted to any bank or lending institution for the purpose of obtaining credit.
F.   List of all securities owned.
G.   List of all insurance policies owned with cash surrender values stated.

Review of the above documents can be critical in identifying assets available for distribution. An examination of cancelled checks might reveal the purchase of municipal bonds (bearer bonds), or investments in undisclosed business ventures of a spouse. Those cancelled checks might also disclose whether or not a wife received, in the past, a specific weekly sum for household expenditures. A review of bank statements (or deposit slips) shows whether or not payroll checks are being deposited into a joint account. If they are, an accountant might find a number of deposits that have gone unaccounted for — which would open up areas of fruitful discovery. Cancelled checks, particularly if drawn to cash, open up areas regarding the source of funds used to maintain a family's lifestyle.

An examination of the individual tax returns filed by the spouse may disclose assets not previously included in answers to interrogatories. The schedule setting forth dividend income may reveal the existence of stock, and assist the accountant in ascertaining whether or not that stock was sold.

Comparative examination of tax returns over five years provides invaluable assistance in demonstrating to a judge, a spouse's ability to pay alimony and child support. An examination of Schedule C of the tax return discloses whether or not the husband has income and expenses from individual ventures.

Where a business is involved, the accountant must examine the books and records of the particular entity, so that he may ascertain the stockholder's equity in the business. Review of the balance sheet might indicate the existence of fixed assets. Although one should not rely upon stated book value or depreciated cost of those fixed assets, areas can be uncovered suggesting that those assets be appraised. After an examination of those records, the accountant should discuss with the attorney the necessity of retaining the services of a business appraiser to value the good will of the business (i.e., excess of the appraised value over net book value).

Although only those assets acquired during the marriage are available for distribution in the event of a divorce, the accountant should make inquiry into assets acquired before the marriage and the status and financial worth of the marital assets, up until the time he issues his report, in order to evaluate a spouse's ability to pay support. The current value of assets are factors considered by the judge in distributing property and by the attorney in settling the case.

Although no one can anticipate the ultimate resolution, the attorney expects his accountant to prepare a schedule showing taxable income and the effect of support payments to each of the parties. It is also prudent to prepare a schedule indicating the tax impact to the parties on various distributions of properties. These schedules are quite helpful in settling matrimonial cases, and assist the trial judge in computing the effects of any decision in terms of net dollars. This can of course, be set forth in a tax trial memo prepared by the accountant in conjunction with the attorney's trial memorandum.

In any professional relationship, and most importantly in a divorce setting, there must be a close dialogue between the attorney, his client, and the accountant. The accountant must be tenacious and ready to go to court and testify if the occasion arises. He must have the patience of Solomon and not be easily discouraged by the many obstacles that will be thrown in his path when he is trying to do his job. He must be diligent, innovative, and resourceful in assisting the attorney and his client in settlement negotiations and litigation.

* *

Mr. Skoloff is Senior Partner, Skoloff & Wolfe, Newark and Morristown, New Jersey; Author, Skoloff, New Jersey Family Law Practice, 5th Edition, 2 volumes; Editor-in-Chief of the Family Advocate, magazine of the American Bar Association, Family Law Section; Editor-in-Chief of the New Jersey Lawyer, official publication of the New Jersey State Bar Association; Treasurer, New Jersey Chapter American Academy of Matrimonial Lawyers; Fellow, American Academy of Matrimonial Lawyers; Member, New Jersey Supreme Court Family Court Committee.

INVESTIGATIVE SERVICES
FOR THE
INSURANCE INDUSTRY

MELVIN I. SHAPIRO, CPA

INTRODUCTION

Throughout the usual work of accountants, there is the constant pressure to follow the principles of GAAP. Audit procedures are prescribed and due adherence to the rules will produce statements of historical results and current fiscal condition, which meet all the criteria. Examinations for the purposes of verifying insurance claims or determining the conditions of a surety bond principal on the verge of or in default, requires departure from the usual audit guidelines in favor of practical and innovative procedures prescribed by the objectives. Instead of true historical circumstances, the auditor may be faced with "what if" conditions presented as potential occurrences to be measured against actual results. Frequently, the examination (fidelity claims) may be concerned with the trail of violations of prescribed internal control procedures. This trail may encompass a myriad of documents and vouchers, which are concentrated within a few balance sheet accounts rather than the financial statement itself. Frequently the auditor may be required to follow and measure physical as well as financial facts. The pressure is on the auditor to be innovative, practical and in tune with the ways of the world to determine the procedures he must use to accomplish the objectives of the case presented by the insurance company. The insurance industry has many different policies covering literally hundreds of potential losses. In this chapter, we will cover the claims that most frequently require auditor involvement: contract surety, fidelity, and business interruption.

CONTRACT SURETY

Before becoming involved in a surety claim, it is advantageous to understand the difference between insurance and surety. Insurance is an agreement to reimburse for losses; it involves a one-to-one relationship. A (the insurance company) agrees to reimburse B (the insured) for losses occurring in defined circumstances. In surety, however, A (the surety) guarantees X (the owner or obligee) that C (the principal) will do a specific thing or perform certain defined tasks; thus a surety bond involves at least three parties. (A surety agreement may also involve dual obligees and joint venturers thus increasing the number of parties but not necessarily the relationships.) The various duties and rights this imposes on the parties are only tangentially the concern of the auditor, and are better left for legal counsel to define. In the case of an insurance claim, once it has paid the claim, the insurance company usually has no further rights of its own and must find "salvage" or reimbursement through the rights of the insured (subrogated rights). In a surety bond situation, any loss suffered by the surety usually constitutes a claim against the principal. In addition, the surety may be entitled to reimbursement for its loss from indemnitors.

The most frequent use of surety bonds is in the construction field where XYZ Surety Company guarantees to LMN Owner, that QRS Construction Company will build a particular structure (within so many days) as set forth in a set of drawings and plans, and "hold LMN Owner harmless" from any claims of laborers, subcontractors, and material providers. To *hold harmless* means that if the construction company fails to pay creditors for services or materials used in the structure the surety will pay all bills incurred in the construction of the building. The obligation by the surety to the owner (obligee) is usually set forth in a document called a Payment and Performance Bond. Frequently, the obligation is included in two documents: a Payment Bond and a Performance Bond. The liability of the insurance company is expressed in dollars and is called *the penal sum.* The penal sum is usually the amount of the contract between the construction company and the owners. Unlike most contracts, the penal sum on the bond can vary as the contract amount changes between the construction company and the owner for extras or deletions, change orders, and backcharges. The surety may not be aware of the variances in the penal sum until a problem arises. However, major swings in the contract price may have some limitations regarding the responsibility of the surety. These limitations are occasionally spelled out in the contract documents but mostly set by the courts in case law. The penal sum may be a fraction of the contract amount rather than the total amount. Thus in some contracts (primarily government projects), the penal sum may be a percentage ranging from 10 to 50% of the construction contract.

Within the last few years, the role of the general contractor has been replaced frequently by a *contract manager* in construction projects. In this form of operation, the contracts that were once written by contractors with subcontractors are (theoretically, at least) written by the owners with the subcontractors directly. In actual practice, however, the contract manager negotiates contracts with the subcontractors. The bond to the owners for payment and performance is still issued. The legal changes in relationships that construction managers have produced, is not usually the concern of the auditor.

The contractor negotiates contracts with specialty contractors (subcontractors) for various functions of the project. The contractor may require from the subcontractor payment and performance bonds. The case presented to the auditors by the surety may be in connection with a default — alleged or actual — of a subcontractor. Most of the following discussion refers to the problems involving a general contractor but relatively, the same work is indicated for a subcontractor.

A considerable amount of construction materials is usually required for the construction project. These may be obtained either by subcontract or by purchase order. Subcontracts for the supply of materials may be bonded, but a purchase order does not usually require a bond from the supplier, particularly if it encompasses "off the shelf" items. Note that the bond issued to the obligee can be used by all project creditors claiming under the principal. Thus, the bond issued by the general contractor to the owner protects everyone who supplies material or labor to the job. A bond supplied by the subcontractor to the general contractor protects the general contractor from claims by any project creditor claiming against the subcontractor. Why would a general contractor require a bond from a subcontractor to protect him against someone who did work for or provided materials to a subcontractor? The owner is liable for payment to *anyone* who supplied labor or material to a job and is unpaid (this is the general rule). This liability is shifted to the general contractor by the contract and the bond. Even where the general contractor has paid the subcontractor, the general contractor is liable to the subcontractor's material suppliers and labor providers (subsubcontractors) if the subcontractor has not made proper payment to them.

To what "tier" does the liability of a contractor (and his surety) extend? At one time it was stated that the contractor's liability did not extend beyond the supplier to the subcontractor's subcontractor, but some recent cases have opened the gates wider and the extent of the liability of the contractor is a matter for legal determination. Where the extent of liability is so broad and so indeterminate on the surface, certain protections have been given to the contractor, who can be severely damaged by claims from those who have been uncompensated by subcontractors for whom they have provided labor or materials or both to a project. The only "protection" accorded the contractor is one of notice; that is the claimant is required to give notice to the one he claims against, within a certain period of time, in order to collect from that person or his surety. The time within which the notice must be given is set forth either in the contract or, if on a Federal project, in an act of Congress called the Miller Act. Most states have adopted acts for State projects which are similar to the Federal Miller Act. These State laws are referred to as Baby Miller Acts. State statutes also prescribe rules for notice which must be complied with if a claimant is seeking payment from one with whom he is not in privity (i.e., a general contractor or his surety in the case of a claimant whose claim derives from a bill to a subcontractor).

We have previously mentioned the terms *extras, deletions, change orders,* and *backcharges*; these are the items which cause the contract price to vary. Extras are items that increase the price of a contract; extras are additions or changes which are decided upon subsequent to the commencement of the work on the project and may or may not be incorporated in a formal change order. Deletions are reductions in a contract which remove or change work to be performed or materials to be provided thereby reducing the price of the project; deletions are usually incorporated in change orders. Change orders are changes made in a project already started; change orders may vary the price of the contract and may be incorporated in the payment schedule of the total project or may be handled as a separate task for payment and performance. Backcharge is a reduction in invoice caused by either the failure in performance which required the payor to perform part of the payee's work, or a charge by the payor to the payee for equipment, labor, materials, etc., which is used to reduce the bill submitted. Change orders may specify a change in the length of time granted the contractor (subcontractor) to complete the project or a phase of it.

We have thus set forth a few of the "rules of the ga
struction, which the auditor must know when he beco
in a surety case. We would assume that the auditor al....,
the rules of construction accounting such that he or she is familiar
with *percentage completion, completed projects,* etc.

Illustration — Construction

Let us now consider the circumstances of a surety case which brings
a call from the surety company for your services. Hasbeen Contractors
is engaged in a number of construction projects for which the Sorry
Surety Company has issued bonds. The contractor also engaged in
jobs that have not required bonding. The surety company has been
receiving a number of notices of nonpayment from subcontractors
and material suppliers on various projects. Until now, the construction company has assured the surety that either they will pay or have
paid the claims, or that they are in dispute with the claimants over
the amount of the invoices or the quality of the service. Now, however, the construction company informs the surety it wants to discuss
the current situation with the surety. The wise surety loss supervisor knows there is trouble and asks the accountants (and legal
counsel) to sit in on the meeting. The contractor at the meeting indicates that its cash flow has been seriously impacted by large overruns in cost on particular jobs and that it requires financial assistance
to complete jobs still on hand. It indicates it has exhausted its bank
credit and the bank, which has duly filed U.C.C. forms for pledges of
the construction equipment, the receivables, and the inventory, is
pressing for note payments now delinquent. The contractor presents
some figures of its current financial condition and the figures on
completion costs. The figures are replete with information on overruns, which are the potential basis for future claims, and claims,
which the contractor feels will be granted but are not now evidenced
by written documents. The wise surety loss supervisor prepares for
signature by the contractor, a request addressed to the Sorry Surety
Company, which states that Hasbeen Contractors is having financial
difficulty in completing its construction contracts and requests the
assistance of the surety company. Upon execution of this document by the contractor the supervisor asks you, as the accountant, to
go to the contractor's office and find out where we stand. This is

where the practice in the field of surety begins. What does "where we stand" imply? Following are the items that we would expect to determine to present to the surety so that the surety can understand the relative size of its exposure and set up appropriate reserves.

A word of caution. The report you present to the surety is the result of your own examination. You are (usually) not reporting on the statements prepared by others so you are not furnishing an audited statement. You are reporting your evaluation of facts and items that 1) have not been confirmed by outside verification; 2) have been only briefly reviewed; 3) are not well documented; 4) require further judgment by experts; 5) are your best judgment at the time of the report but may require further examination. In your letter of transmittal, mention these qualifications and emphasize that the objective is to give an estimate, an approximation, a current determination, or such other terms that make it expressly clear that you are not attempting a definitive evaluation.

Prepare Schedules

Schedules of the following should be presented. These schedules are to be submitted by jobs.

1. Original contract price.
2. Change orders.
3. Revised contract amount.
4. Work already billed.
5. Balance available (unbilled) on contracts.
6. Requisitions and retainages unpaid.
7. Total funds available.
8. Estimated cost to complete.
9. Payables.
10. Total requirements.
11. Shortfalls.
12. Overages.

Let us examine the various items involved. The schedules should be divided into *bonded jobs* and *unbonded jobs* and should be listed by bond number. Usually the schedules will also include the contractor's project numbers and a brief description of the job. An unbonded job is a job not bonded by the surety company that has engaged you. It may be bonded by another surety company, but it is not the problem of your client.

1. The *original contract price* is determined by referring to the original contract. The amount of the contract and the amount of the bond should be the same if it is a 100% bonded project. While looking at the contracts it is advisable to scan them for various pertinent items, which should be noted on a general review sheet for each contract. Pertinent information on each contract, in addition to the contract amount, includes: parties to the contract; date executed; date set for completion; liquidated damages provisions, if any, for delay; definitions of completion or "substantial completion"; retainage provisions; date requisitions are to be submitted; approval time; payment time; requirements for arbitration; names of architects and engineers, etc.

2. *Change orders* should be listed in three categories: those approved and documented, those that correspondence indicates will definitely be granted and are merely awaiting documentation, and those represented by "request for pricing" received from owner and other correspondence, but are not indicated as granted. Also included in this last category are claims by the contractor for extras or changes which he feels he should be awarded but for which he has not been awarded. These should not be included in your initial report in the amount available to complete the project but rather in a note for future discussion.

   A schedule should be presented of the change orders (divided into the above categories). Since the accountant is going to make a judgment as to what he or she will add to the original contract amount for change orders from the second category, he should qualify the items that are in any way questionable by indicating that he has used his best judgment. We will state here that we are expected to use our best judgment and should be reasonable, rational, and logical, rather than legalistic.

Let us review the objectives of your examination at this point. You are trying to give the surety some basis for *estimating* the probable exposure. Usually the dollar amounts in a surety loss situation are large. The surety loss supervisor is not looking to you for exact amounts; he has others to depend upon as well: legal counsel, engineers, etc. Your objective is to provide as much information as possible to assist all parties. You can make an incorrect judgment; but as long as you provide the background and reasons for your judgment you will not be deemed negligent for an estimate later found to be incorrect.

Although they would constitute a point of reference, note that the basic books of account have not been suggested as the source of the information you are presenting; you have used original documents! You would of course, check the jobs on hand with cost records, but your first resource is the documents themselves, if available.

3. The *revised contract amount* is the aggregate (by contract) of the original contract and the change orders. Note that the reason you set out both the original contract and the revision is that the surety may want to take a (legal) position that the number of change orders releases the surety from liability because of a (legal) defense called *novation*. The reason for listing the change orders that produced the amended sum is to permit the surety to determine whether the *quantity* of change orders is such that an extension of the time is required for completion, or to permit the surety to assess the change orders as a factor in warranting a delay claim by the contractor.

4. *Work already billed* can be determined from the requisitions. It is good procedure to tabulate all the requisitions on each job by date, amount, etc. A valuable fact, which may or may not be shown on the requisitions and which may require reference to the receipts book, is the date of payment received on each requisition. The comparison of date submitted, date approved, and date paid may be pertinent in a claim by the contractor alleging that the owner has not fulfilled his obligations under the contract.

5. *Balance available* is the amount obtained by subtracting the amount of work already billed (4) from the revised contract amount (3). This item is sometimes designated "Unbilled Balance on Contract" or "Contract Balance."

6. *Requisitions and retainages unpaid* are usually shown on your schedules separately, because of the timing differences in

collection. Requisitions are the periodic billings for work done after subtracting retainage amounts as provided in the contract. Retainages and requisition amounts can usually be determined from the requisitions. These figures should be checked to the books of account, but this might be difficult because of timing. The requisitions are probably a sufficiently accurate source. Compare requisitions with amounts recorded in the receipts book.

In addition to jobs currently in process, there may be jobs that are substantially complete or previously completed. These should be included in your exposure schedule because not only are there probably retainages and requisition receivables outstanding, but (more importantly) there will probably be payables outstanding. The time from the last requisition or bill for retainage to the present should be noted for each such item. An extended period from the time of requisition to the current time might indicate that the job is not accepted or only partially so, which could be a booby trap for the surety if the job is bonded. In fact, it is a good idea to discuss each completed but unpaid job with management. Note especially any jobs that are in suit or about to be entered in court. Review legal files!

7. The aggregate of unbilled balances on contract, requisitions receivable, and unpaid retainage is the *total funds available* to complete the contract. Note that we could subtract from the revised contract amount (Item 3) the amount collected to date (a figure available, usually, on the requisition) and come up with the amount available on the contract, without splitting it into the three parts: unbilled, retainage, and requisition. Why did we go to the trouble? Remember the bank? In some jurisdictions it has been held that billings for completed work (requisitions) are not available to the surety for payment and completion against a creditor who has duly made a U.C.C. (Uniform Commerical Code) filing. It would not be within the accountant's purview to make the legal decision concerning the rights of the bank versus the surety. Give the breakdown and let the lawyers resolve the issue. (Generally, any amounts unpaid on a bonded project are available to the surety to complete and pay for the project.)

At this point, it has been determined how much is available to complete and pay for the project. It is now incumbent on the accountant to determine what it is going to cost to do so.

8. *Estimated cost to complete* is an engineering item. Without considerable experience in the construction business, an accountant has no expertise to permit him to project, with accuracy, the amounts of labor, material, and subcontract work required for final acceptance of the work. Remember that management's estimates are probably inadequate. (The contractor would probably not be in difficulty if he had been accurate in his estimations of costs.) However, an engineering estimate of the cost will probably not be available for weeks, and your client is anxiously waiting for your "statement of exposure" — so go ahead and venture an estimate of the cost to complete the project.

In today's construction industry, anywhere from 60%–80% of projects are subcontracted or purchase ordered. Thus, assuming that the predicament of the contractor has not produced a termination of the contracts with the subcontractors and the vendors, you must worry about only 40%–20% of a contract — your margin of error.

Assuming that a substantial part of the work has been done, then your margin of error is even less. You also may have some materials to work with: original estimates, C.P.M.'s (Critical Path Method of scheduling), PERT charts (Program Evaluation Review Technique), bar graphs, etc. If you understand these techniques and can read and evaluate the charts, use them; if not, just try to estimate by using common sense. You may use the contractor's own estimate. In any event, qualify your estimate by stating emphatically that it is *your* estimate and is to be used only for the limited purpose of the report and is not really within the sphere of competence of an accountant.

Let us say the contractor bid $1,000,000 for a job, assuming it was going to cost $900,000. Of the $900,000, $600,000 (66 2/3%) was contracted out. Included in the $300,000 of work left for the contractor to provide that you must be concerned about, are errors in judgment made by the principal (unit prices), omission of items in the original estimate, excessive costs, etc. After a few cases in the construction industry, you will get a feel for the competence of the management of the company. Suppose for various reasons, some of which are intuitive, you figure this is a "20% error company." You estimate the error factor of the $900,000 at 20% so that the cost of completion is estimated as follows:

	Contract Amount	Billed	Balance
Subcontractors	$ 500,000	$300,000	$200,000
Material	100,000	40,000	60,000
Own Work	300,000	160,000	–
Contingency (20%)	180,000	–	320,000
	$1,080,000	$500,000	$580,000

You may want to add a further contingency to the figure. Do *not* furnish the computation in the report! Furnish the figure and note your qualification but do not indicate how you arrived at the amount. (After many engagements with insurance companies, the accuracy of your estimate of completion costs becomes an item for mutual "ragging.") There is a second component of "cost to complete," which also involves a tremendous amount of imagination and expertise to determine. This is the *overhead* necessary for the period from the time of engagement to the completion of all jobs. This involves time frames for overhead personnel, estimates to termination date of office rental equipment and services, office materials and supplies necessary, rent, telephone, etc. Management services will be an item to be determined. Overhead may be assigned to individual projects on the basis of construction costs to complete. Other bases may be used provided they carry a logical reason for use. Any funds on deposit in the account of the contractor not earmarked for specific jobs should be shown as available to defer current overhead payables and future overhead costs.

Whether the surety will finance the contractor to completion or whether it will terminate this contractor in whole or in part will be determined in good measure by comparison between the cost to complete as computed (including overhead) with bids from other contractors for "turnkey" or other types of contracts. Whereas the engineers will determine the projected costs of construction to completion, it will be up to you to compute the cost of overhead to completion dates furnished by the engineers. Be imaginative, reasonable and conservative in estimating overhead.

9. *Payables* probably consume the greatest amount of examination time by the accountants. Payables involve amounts due subcontractors on retainage and on requisition, payables due for overhead, and claims against the contractor on both current and completed jobs. A schedule of subcontractors would be advisable showing the number of contracts, the change orders, the accepted billings, the amounts due on retainage, the amounts due on requisition, the disputed change orders, the extras, the backcharges. If possible, a schedule of purchase order status would also be in order. In creating the schedules, the books of account would probably be helpful, if accurate. Remember that payables must be set forth by jobs, since the liability of the surety extends only to bonded jobs and each bonded job may involve for the surety a different group of reinsurers.

If the purchase register or the accounts payable ledger is set up so that payables are maintained by jobs, the work is considerably less. But if no attempt has been made by the contractor to separate payables by job, the long, tedious job of reviewing invoices and assigning the costs to particular jobs cannot be avoided. If job cost records are maintained, this source of allocation to jobs might be helpful in conjunction with invoices. Where a multitude of projects are in a substantially completed or completed status and reflect payables due on them, we have the secondary task of determining whether they are payables which are the responsibility of the surety. Remember the requirements of notice to qualify under the bond that was mentioned earlier? In listing the payables it is a good idea to indicate the date and amounts of the last billings by the creditor. It would also be helpful to set forth the original contract amount of the subcontracts. This list of payables by jobs should be a separate schedule since it will be the basis used by legal counsel, in the absence of other data, to determine whether the surety is liable to the creditor on the basis of due notice.

Circumstances will be encountered where shipments made by the creditor to several projects can be allocated to projects but payments in lump sum or in round amounts have been made to the creditor. Of course, if the invoices being paid are designated on the remittance, finding the balance of payables by jobs is expedited. If no allocation to invoices has been made, the creditor, in many jurisdictions, may apply remittances as it sees fit. (Naturally, it will apply payments to nonbonded jobs first.) Generally, you will use a first-in, first-out approach. Of course, if there is some notice *to the creditor* that the funds were derived from a particular project, the invoices from that project will be eliminated first.

When engineers or contract loss claim managers compute the cost to complete a project, they frequently include unpaid requisitions and retainage as part of the cost to complete. If you adopt this procedure you will have difficulty in computing cash flow requirements and bases for defending claims.

10. *Total requirements* are of course the sum of costs to complete the construction plus the payables; it would also include projected overhead. It should represent the total amount required to terminate all projects presently on the books of the contractor.

11. *Shortfalls* include all projects in which the difference between the amount available (Item 5) is less than the requirements (Item 10). The aggregate of the amounts on bonded jobs in this column is the exposure of the surety company.

12. *Overages* include all projects in which the amount shown as available (Item 5) exceeds the requirements (Item 10). Ordinarily there is no offset between shortfall and overages unless the surety assumes all liabilities and the obligation to complete all jobs. If the contractor is in bankruptcy, the overages are available to the court for administrative expenses, etc. Remember the bank with a UCC filing on receivables? The overages would be available to satisfy the bank's claim. Any excess after satisfying the bank or other creditor secured by contract balances would be available to satisfy claims of nonbonded creditors (including the bonding company to the extent that it is a general creditor for its losses as set forth in the shortfall column).

The items set forth above, lead to a number of subsidiary schedules. It is a first report together with or followed shortly by the list of creditors by job. The surety must have these schedules to determine, in the first instance (from the exposure schedule), what courses of action to pursue and, from the payable schedules, what pressing creditors with warranted claims can, in some states, subject the surety to penalties. It is the accountant's objective to give the surety the information as soon as possible.

Additional Work

Other work may be requested from the accountant by the surety. If the surety decides to finance the contractor to completion, the accountant may be required to furnish cash flow projections and to monitor expenditures. This requires close cooperation with engineers. If the work to be done is sufficiently large and protracted, it may be advisable to develop a data processing program for this purpose. If the contractor already has equipment it may require modifications of programs or adaptation to the new circumstances.

Another task that the accountant may be requested to do which involves considerable time involves the determination of excess costs which may constitute the basis of "delay claims." The accountant may be requested to assist in working out finance arrangements for the use of equipment, deferral of notes, arrangements with banks, etc.

The accountant may be requested to furnish a list of the contractor's assets available for sale. The books of account, particularly the fixed asset schedules, are a point of departure. But remember that historical cost may have little correspondence to current costs. Another caveat is the possibility that some fixed assets belonging to the contractor may have been charged off to particular jobs. This is permissible under some large government jobs and some (large) private jobs. It is advisable to use experts as well as trade manuals to determine valuations.

In addition to the construction surety loss claims discussed above, there are other forms of surety losses that may be assigned to the accountant. These include customs bonds, bulk mail delivery bonds, and other guarantees of performance designated as "miscellaneous" surety bonds.

Work on surety losses can be extremely interesting and remunerative. This type of work breaks the pattern of the usual accounting engagements and is an exciting challenge. Remember though, that the keys are common sense, creativity, and innovation.

FIDELITY

Experience in fidelity loss claims for insurance companies can provide vivid examples of the effects of poor internal control. Such examples may be used in teaching staff. The methods used by employees to divert funds are factual examples of the results of poor supervision, failure of standard operating procedures, or circumvention of well conceived controls.

The parties to a fidelity loss are the insured, frequently designated as an *obligee*, the employee culprit usually called the *principal* or the *obligor*, and the insurance company. The obligation by the insurance company to reimburse the insured is contained in any of a number of policies. It can be covered in an Employee Fidelity Bond, a policy covering Dishonesty, Disappearance and Destruction (usually called a "3-D" policy), or any of a number of blanket bonds such as a Banker's Blanket Bond, etc.

A common feature of fidelity bond coverage is a *deductible*. A deductible is the amount the insured must bear of the loss before the insurance company reimburses. The policies usually carry maximum limits of the insurance company's liability.

Unlike surety bonds, which guarantee a particular project and can run for an indefinite period depending on the length of the project, a fidelity bond is usually for a specific period. The period defines the length of time during which a loss may be discovered and claimed for reimbursement from the insurance company, or the period during which the loss occurred for which the insurance company will be liable. It is possible to be covered for both in the change over of insurance carriers and coverages, but a waiver (endorsement) is required for protection. Some suggested procedures regarding fidelity loss engagements are as follows:

1. Read the policy and endorsements under which the insured is claiming. Note the designation of the person covered by the policy. Employees are usually covered but frequently officer/ employees are not. In some cases, representatives or agents are covered; in this case the description of the relationship that constitutes a covered representative or agent is extremely important. Is the insurance company liable for only losses *discovered* during the specific period or for losses that

occurred during the period? Within what period after discovery of a loss must the insured notify the company?

2. Read the claim (usually designated a "Proof of Loss"). How
   many employees are claimed to be involved? Were there
   outsiders involved? Are actual employees named or is it a
   case of mysterious disappearance? Is it a merchandise loss
   claim or a cash loss claim? Does it allege a benefit to the
   obligor? Were the police involved? Is there an admission
   (confession)?

3. When writing a report, preliminary or final, do not make legal
   determinations. The malfeasance claimed is always the
   alleged or _claimed_ malfeasance or diversion; the person cited
   is the alleged malfeasor.

4. Do not put in writing any speculations you may have that
   appear to justify the claim. If you feel there are some items
   of merit in the claim or that the claim is warranted but you
   do not have total justification, convey the feeling and your
   basis for it orally. The reason for this is that, under present
   law, your report will probably be available to the claimant
   and his counsel in case of litigation in discovery procedures
   and your words may be taken out of the total context. Of
   course, if your investigation shows that the _facts_ indicate the
   claim is valid, you will so state. Let us take some situations
   and apply them.

Inventory Shortage

ABC Company finds a huge shortage in its inventory based on its
comparison of physical findings with book findings. The investigation discovers that the inventory manager is gambling heavily, living
beyond his means, staying after hours each night, and has purchased
a station wagon. (He has the only access to the warehouse after
hours.) If you have read the policy of coverage you will find under
claims exclusion (usually 2(b)) that (most policies state) any loss, the
fact or amount of which has been determined by reference to an inventory or profit and loss statement, can not be the basis of a claim.
Through frequent cases in court, and as included presently in policy
wording, this clause has been interpreted to mean that if other evidence
is available that proves that an employee has diverted merchandise to

his own use or benefit, then reference can be made to the inventory to determine the *amount* of the loss. Thus the mere fact of inventory shortage cannot be the basis of a claim unless it can be shown by other evidence that the employee actually diverted inventory for his own use. Although the activities cited may link the inventory manager to the shortage, the ABC Company must prove that the employee actually diverted inventory for his own use. From then on, it is incumbent on the accountant to determine what part of the inventory shortage is attributable to the employee — How accurate was the book inventory? What were the shortages in prior years? What kinds and amounts of adjustments were made during the period?

Bank Loans

John C. is a loan officer in a bank. His authority is limited to $10,000 of loans to any one borrower. To increase the business of the bank, John makes 25 loans to various people in the aggregate amount of $200,000, knowing that all the loans are controlled by one individual using other people as fronts. Of course the individual was credit worthy! But the individual proves worthless and the loans are in default. The bank claims a loss under its bankers blanket bond. First, you note that there is a $25,000 deductible per individual. Then the form of the bond is examined. In 1976, the bankers blanket bond was revised so that a new definition of covered dishonesty was promulgated. A covered loss is a loss caused by an employee who commits the act for either his or her own direct or indirect personal economic benefit (excluding incentive bonuses for good performance), or to deliberately harm the bank. Was the bank entitled to collect under the bond in John's exceeding his authority? The answer is the problem of legal counsel once the accountant has verified the dollar loss.

Receivables

George B. is charged with collecting receivables. His instructions are that when loans are over 60 days past due, he must furnish an aged list to his supervisor. George is negligent and fails to do so. The company suffers high amounts of losses on its receivables. You analyze the losses and find that some of the losses are represented by accounts that are customarily given longer terms by company policy (some of the accounts were insolvent when shipped, etc). Your judgment? The insurance company did not insure the credit of the customers. George did not gain personally from the transactions. Was the loss a credit loss, or a fidelity loss?

Inventory Shortage

Henry D. was a warehouse employee. On three successive nights he was seen by another employee loading merchandise from the warehouse into his station wagon. It was also proved that the three nights were the only nights where, under Henry's inducements, the night security man left the premises for two hours each night. Confronted with witnesses, Henry breaks down and confesses to the entire inventory shortage of $58,000. From experience you know that frequently when a malfeasor is caught he confesses to anything and everything, impelled by the release of the tension of concealment. It is the mission of the accountant to separate fact from fiction in the admission. Here, the accountant leaves his usual field of books and financial figures and becomes realistic and innovative. Some basic facts and figures are available. The length of time available for the theft is known (6 hours). The number of trips can be estimated. The size of the vehicle can be measured. The size of the merchandise is measurable. From these facts it is possible to prove the maximum physical quantity of merchandise that could be moved. From here it is an easy step to determine the value of the merchandise that Henry could have removed. It is considerably less than the amount in the confession. With this as a guide, the insurance company can make a settlement with the insured at considerably less than the confessed amount.

Determining Cost

The S Steel Company through its internal security forces, intercepts an unauthorized shipment of steel being diverted from one of its plants to one of the customers of the steel company, who was paying the employees on a fixed price per load for the steel. By surveying the records at various weigh stations, the company finds that the pattern of theft had been continuing for some time. The specific amount of diverted steel is determined. The cost value of the steel is determined from the company's records, and the company files a sizable claim with the insurance company. An accountant was engaged by the insurance company to verify the calculations. The accountant had little, if any, quarrel with the quantity of steel but had considerable problems with the claimed cost value. The costing procedures of the company required detailed examination. It found that the company sold two classes of steel, called *primary* and *secondary*. Primary steel was steel manufactured to specifications submitted by the customer. Overruns on the customer's order would constitute secondary steel and would be stacked in the yard with steel from other overruns and miscellaneous steel from other sources. The diverted steel was determined to be secondary steel. Secondary steel would carry relatively the same cost basis on the company's books as primary steel. While primary steel was sold at a profit, secondary steel was sold at a loss since, not being manufactured to exact specifications of the steel purchaser, it was considerably lower priced. The customer, in effect, took "potluck" in his purchases from the piles of steel on the yard.

The accountant challenged the policy of the company for assigning the cost of secondary steel. Note that the problems of consistency and uniformity according to GAAP are not the problem of the insurance company's investigating accountant. The question is the *actual* value of the secondary steel. To the accountant, the fact that it was consistently sold below book value indicated that the secondary steel was certainly not worth the book value. The accountant suggested a cost value determined by averaging gross profit realized over the past several years on combined sales of primary and secondary steel, and allocating the cost between the two grades so that the primary steel gross profit was reduced and the secondary steel sales produced a nominal gross profit. This reduced the claim of the steel company by some 60%. After considerable negotiation the steel company agreed to reduce its claim to less than 50% of the original amount claimed and the case was settled.

Diverting Funds

A bank teller in charge of automatic teller machines was diverting funds from the bank by manipulating vouchers. When funds were received through deposits to an ATM (Automated Teller Machine) the teller would prepare the duplicate vouchers called for by standard operating procedures, but would turn only one copy in to the cashier. He would hold the other (debit) copy for 14 days and then replace it with a duplicate from another set of forged vouchers, holding the duplicate (credit) for another 14 days. This procedure was carried on for several years resulting in larger and larger amounts of fund diversions and increased discrepancies in depositors' accounts. The 14 day period was the time frame for matching vouchers under the procedures of the head cashier. The head cashier retired. The new cashier thought the 14 day period was excessive and ordered the time span cut to three days. The teller could not create the paperwork necessary in so short a time and his diversion was exposed. The teller admitted to diversion of *all* shortages in all funds in the bank's accounts. This required considerable work for the surety company's accountants. The trail of the diversion involved thousands of vouchers and a myriad of records. The diversion involved some 14 branches of the bank which had been receiving deposits through automatic teller machines. Although the loss was large, the cost effectiveness of tracing the diversion from the original vouchers through to the end was questionable, in terms of its potential accuracy and its doubtful conclusion. What the accountant did was to start at the end with the shortage of funds in effect at the denouement and work backwards for a reasonable period eliminating all items that did not appear to be part of the stream of diversion. This was used as a basis for percentage reduction of the amount of loss from the teller's alleged diversion. Then, an examination of the amount of relative bank shortages over the years was determined and used to further reduce the loss claim presented. This reduced amount was offered to the bank in settlement. The final figure of settlement was negotiated between the bank and the surety company using the accountant's calculations as a basis.

Consequential Losses

One of the frequent sources of controversy in fidelity losses is what is usually termed *consequential* losses. For instance, suppose the employee diverts to his own use, $100,000 of remittances from an important customer, who consequently becomes so incensed by the dunning letters he receives that he terminates his business with the insured. Consequently, the company goes into bankruptcy, having sustained a million dollar loss. Would the insurance company be liable for $100,000 or $1,000,000? The $1,000,000 loss would probably be deemed a consequential (noncompensible) loss. (This might be altered if the delinquency of the surety in paying the $100,000 loss produced the $1,000,000 loss — but this derives from other than the fidelity bond.)

Many bonds preclude from recovery, prospective income from diverted funds. This has frequently been interpreted to mean that interest accrued on fraudulent loans by banks are not to be reimbursed under the financial blanket bonds. This produces an interesting problem for the accountant where fraudulent loans have been moved from one form of loan to another, and interest has been added to principal from time to time.

The preceding cases are used to indicate the variety and complexity of cases that the fidelity loss claim field presents to the accountant. Note that in many instances the exact amount of loss to be reimbursed is a matter of negotiation; the accountant will adopt a theory for determining the amount or extent of the loss, which may be disputed by the claimant. The accountant's theory should be logical, reasonable, and sustainable in law, since he may be called upon to justify his approach in a court procedure on the claim. The accountant should be cost conscious in his approach to the case. While claims managers want to pay no more than the claims warrant, they do not want Pyrrhic victories whereby the expenses of examination and litigation exceed the claim reduction.

BUSINESS INTERRUPTION

Although there is a policy commonly issued by insurance companies called a Business Interruption policy, there are numerous situations where claims are made under other forms of coverage for loss of profits due to cessation or suspension of business. Thus, engineer malpractice claims may involve losses due to business interruption; and workmen's compensation claims may involve losses due to the inability to perform services during a particular period. Basically, the problems in all these types of claims are the same and involve a "what if" situation: What if the suspension had not occurred? What would the operating results of the business have been? The accountant in this type of situation must rely on historical facts and common sense.

The Business Interruption policy is usually written in conjunction with a fire or similar policy involving destruction of property. One of the primary caveats is the separation of recompense for the loss of property from the recompense from the results of the suspension of business. The claimant is to be recompensed under a business interruption policy for the loss of the profits he would have made if the business had not been suspended. If the business had been operating at a loss, it is the amount of loss sustained which exceeded the loss that would have been sustained if no interruption had occurred. The first determination to be made is the length of time it would take under normal and reasonable procedures for the business to be back in full swing. Note that the business interruption policy usually provides that the insured will be reimbursed for unusual expenditures to expedite the business recovery or to reduce the amount of loss sustained during the period. However, the amount of such unusual expenditures must not exceed the amount of loss that would have been sustained if the expenditures had not been made and the recovery period had run its course. In other words, expenditures, which reduce the loss, are compensable, but the limit of loss is the amount which would have been sustained if no heriocs had been used.

Losses under business interruption policies begin with the gross profit. From the gross profit there is deducted, those expenses that would be eliminated by the suspension of business. The primary source of dispute in this instance is personnel payments. The insured will claim that he could not subsequently replace certain key or trained personnel if he dispenses with their services. Another source of dispute may be advertising costs. On the other hand, part of the heroics to reduce losses may be increased advertising. The payment of high rents for warehouse or office space in the interim may be a source of dispute or may be claimed as a factor in reducing losses.

In determining the amount of loss on the "what if" the suspension had not occurred situation, actual historical results would be projected into the future. It behooves the accountant to analyze the business and separate operations into components. Analysis of the various components of the operations may reveal facts that indicate trends which affect the pattern of growth (or decline) of the business.

Within the components there may be spurts of sales volume produced on a temporal basis, which could not be expected to be sustained during the suspension period. Costs affecting gross profit may have been beneficially affected during historical periods, which might not be available during the suspension period. Projections previously prepared routinely for management covering the suspension period would be relevant. Comparison of actual results with experienced results projected for the period unaffected by the suspension would help to evaluate the reliability of the projections for use in determining the results during the suspended period.

It is helpful to the claims adjuster if a bar, a line, or another projection of the calculations could be furnished in the accountant's report. This is easily done now with computers by making a graph of projections calculated by the accountant's examination. In fact, the interpolation of figures for the report is considerably expedited by the use of computers.

The loss covered by the Business Interruption policy, like most other coverages, does not cover secondary or consequential losses. If, because of the suspension of business, the insured loses its place in the industry, the losses subsequent to the suspension period, which were produced by the loss of position in the industry, are generally not covered. The profit on a contract not awarded during the period, which would have been performed in a subsequent period, is usually not a direct loss covered by the policy. The accountant is faced with the need to make these kinds of determinations in his analysis of the claim.

In facing a loss covered by a workmen's compensation claim, or an engineering malpractice claim, substantially the same approach as in Business Interruption claims would be taken by the accountant in measuring lost profits. In the case of the engineer's malpractice claim, however, the ramification of losses may be far greater. In Business Interruption claims or Workmen's Compensation claims, the basis of reimbursement is usually determined by the pattern and trend of historical earnings. While this may also be the primary basis of a claim in the engineering malpractice case, it may arise from entirely different sources. The claim may arise from the lack of use of a brand new facility. This requires projection of profits for a situation in which there is no historical background. There may also be claims for physical damage which require valuation calculations.

The accountant for the insurance company has the advantage, to some extent, of being presented with the thoughts of the claimant, who has attacked the problem and submitted the claim based on what he considers viable premises. The accountant may seek flaws in either the calculations of the claimant or the basic premise used. If the latter is the line the accountant takes, he should be prepared to offer an approach based on other reasonable, defensible, economically based premises, or at least be prepared to point out the inconsistencies of the approach used by the insured in presenting his claim. Obviously, there can be no set rules for the accountant in approaching these claims. Experience in business affairs, and recognition of analogous situations which might be helpful, are the accountant's best tools.

* *

Melvin I. Shapiro is a Certified Public Accountant and a member of the Massachusetts and the Federal Bar. He practices as a partner in the accounting firm of Tofias, Fleishman, Shapiro & Company, of Boston, and heads its litigation support department. For many years, Mr. Shapiro has been active in the fields of surety, loss claims, and fidelity cases. He has also acted as an arbitrator and an expert witness in construction disputes. Mr. Shapiro has achieved a national reputation in the field, and is frequently called upon to address meetings of underwriters, bankers, attorneys, and construction executives.

APPENDICES

APPENDIX A

CHRONOLOGY OF A CASE

Let us run through a hypothetical but thoroughly likely scenario of how one of these investigative assignments might work. This involves a matrimonial case where we are contacted by an attorney to represent the wife.

Day 1. Attorney contacts us by phone to indicate that he or she has an interesting matrimonial job and feels that our services are needed.

Day 2. We issue a letter to the attorney advising of our requirements in terms of money, certain timeframes, and record discovery (without getting specific).

Day 10. Not having heard anything yet, we follow-up by telephone, and find out that the client (the wife, in this case) still hasn't made up her mind.

Day 20. The wife decides that it is the right move to engage us and gives the attorney the go ahead. The attorney then contacts us and a brief conversation ensues. It is agreed that we will meet the wife, in the normal course of our interview function, to initiate our services. We call the wife to arrange for an interview. She is not it, and we leave a message.

Day 22. The wife calls us back and advises that she's having some second thoughts as to working with the present attorney and would like to hold off on anything further. We call the attorney who originally contacted us. That attorney is out at a trial, so we leave a message to return the call.

Day 24. The attorney calls us back and advises that he or she is aware of the situation, and that we all must be patient.

Day 35. The wife gives us a call, and says that she has decided to stay with the present attorney, has advised the attorney of same, and would now like to meet with us. We set an appointment date for four days hence.

Day 36. We have our standard engagement letter prepared to present to the wife when we meet with her; and also have prepared and mailed to the appropriate parties our standard records discovery letter asking for access to various books and records of the businesses to be investigated.

Day 38. We get a call from the wife advising that a personal problem has occurred — she cannot keep the following day's appointment, and would like to reschedule it. I am not in the office at the time and, therefore, my secretary takes the message for me to return her call.

Day 39. I call the wife, and reschedule the appointment for three days hence.

Day 42. We have a conference with the wife, during which we give her the engagement letter and ask that she review it and, within the next couple of days, return a signed copy along with our retainer check. We also contact (for instance) the husband's attorney to follow up our records request letter and to obtain access to the books and records of the business. The husband's attorney is not in, but will return our call.

Day 44. Having received no return call from the husband's attorney, we follow up with another telephone call and also call the wife's attorney to advise of our progress.

Day 46. Husband's attorney calls and advises that she has no problem with our investigating the business, but we should contact the husband's accountant to arrange details. We do so immediately. The accountant is not in; he will return our call.

Day 48. Husband's accountant calls us and explains that he knows we're involved, but has no idea of what records we want to see. Apparently, he was never given a copy of our letter. We send him one immediately.

Day 51. We contact the husband's accountant to follow up the records discovery letter, and set up an appointment with him. The earliest date available that's mutually agreeable and allows for gathering of the records is approximately two weeks hence.

IT SHOULD BE NOTED THAT OVER 50 DAYS HAD ELAPSED SINCE FIRST BEING CONTACTED BEFORE WE COULD ESTABLISH A DATE TO BEGIN OUR FIELDWORK — AND THAT DATE WAS 65 DAYS AFTER THE INITIAL CONTACT. Although we prefer to receive tax returns and financial statements in advance of our going in, the practicalities of the situation do not permit such.

Day 65. We get to the husband's business to begin our work, and find that not all of the business records we've asked for are present, and none of the personal records are there — his accountant didn't have control over these records (that is often the case) and the husband is not available. We do our work and, at the end of that day, leave a list of follow-up items and records needed.

Day 66. We send a follow-up letter to all parties concerned advising of our additional record requirements and requesting a return date.

Day 70. We make appropriate telephone calls to follow up the status of our returning to resume our investigative work. We follow up these telephone calls with correspondence to put same on record.

Day 74.   The husband's accountant calls us, and we arrange a resumption of the investigative work at the next mutually available dates — 13 and 16 days from now.

Day 87 and 90.   We work these two days at the husband's business, and, except for a few follow-up questions, complete all field work.

Day 91.   Correspondence to follow up open questions is issued, and a prompt reply requested. We also call the wife and arrange for another interview to go over various findings and get further input from her — now that we have solid information.

Day 101.   Replies to our questions are received.

Day 105.   We have a conference with the wife, discuss our findings, and get further insight from her.

Day 112.   Before putting our preliminary findings in a report, we contact the attorney and the wife to discuss those findings.

Day 116.   We prepare a preliminary draft of our report.

Day 117.   After the first typing transcription, report is edited, polished, and returned for retyping.

Day 119.   The report is ready and, after getting the okay, mailed to the wife's attorney, the wife, and the wife's business appraiser.

Day 127.   Both the wife's attorney and the wife get back to us to establish a conference. Date is set nine days hence — the first mutually agreeable date for all three parties.

Day 131.   Court date set for day 162.

Day 136.   Conference with attorney and wife.

Day 138.   Preliminary report revision, and put in for typing.

Day 140.   Report edited and polished.

Day 141.   Report finished — issued to the attorney, the wife, and the business appraiser.

Note that 141 days have passed — nearly 5 months — and it has taken this long with all due diligence and without any extraordinary or unusual delays caused by either side. We have now submitted the report to the appraiser. We're not even up to the point where the husband and his attorney and expert have had the chance to review the report, critique it, and use it in any negotiations.

Day 155.   Husband's attorney contacts wife's attorney indicating that she wishes to depose me. On the same date, wife's attorney contacts me, by phone, to advise of this, and asks for acceptable dates on my part. These dates must obviously be coordinated with not just the wife's attorney and the husband's attorney but also, most typically, with at least one or two of the husband's experts, and in some cases perhaps, with the husband and also the wife. It can be a regular circus as to who's attending.

Day 156. Wife's attorney issues a letter to me advising of our previous telephone conversation (copying husband's attorney); and I issue a similar letter confirming my end of the conversation and suggested dates.

Day 160. Multiple telephone calls back and forth between numerous parties to establish a deposition date. Issue mutually deferred pending scheduled court date two days hence.

Day 161. Court date rescheduled (to accommodate case status) to day 166.

Day 166. Attorneys in judge's chambers receive tongue lashing and pressured to settle. No movement results. Court date rescheduled to day 189 (the first available date on a crowded court calendar).

Day 168. Resumption of multiple calls to establish a deposition date. Date is set for six days later.

Day 173. Two of the parties involved in the depositions call to advise that something has come up, they cannot attend, and therefore, the depositions must be postponed.

Day 175. Multiple telephone calls to rearrange deposition date. Various parties unreachable, and return calls will have to be made.

Day 177. Return calls made and again multiple telephone calls to establish a mutually agreeable date for depositions. Date is established eight days from now.

Day 185. My deposition.

Day 189. Court date rescheduled to day 215 — too many cases originally scheduled for this date, and most don't settle, forcing mass postponements.

Day 197. Appraiser's report is issued.

Day 203. Telephone calls begin to establish conference date with appraiser.

Day 204. Return calls to establish date with appraiser. Date established five days hence.

Day 209. Conference with attorney, wife, appraiser, and accountant.

Day 215. Attorneys in judge's chambers advise judge of some progress and potential movement towards settlement. Court date rescheduled (court calender crowded) to day 242.

Day 216. Telephone discussion with wife's attorney on various matters involved in this case.

Day 219. Telephone calls with appraiser and wife on various matters involved in this case.

Day 223. Telephone calls with wife's attorney involving matters in this case.

Day 229. Negotiations.

Days 231–241. Frequent and multiple telephone calls between numerous parties to discuss fine points and schedule and reschedule pretrial conferences and negotiation settlements.

Day 242. Case settled.

The preceding was a very real chronology (except for the frequently occurring, intentional stalling not included herein) of a typical case and illustrates what is involved from the time you are first contacted as the investigative accountant, to the time the case is settled — which, without any serious complications or stalling by either side, can easily run eight months. It doesn't matter that this case might not have been particularly big or complicated — all the calls and conferences and correspondence described are typical for virtually any case. A bigger case will generally involve more time, but a smaller case will not require appreciably less time. For instance, in a case where there's a reasonable attempt to prevent you from walking in the door to begin your investigation, you can well add six months to a year to the timeframe described above. The author has been involved in more than one case that ran between one and two years, and even longer, from the time of his involvement to the time the case was settled. Keep in mind that my involvement was not the beginning of the case.

Other reasons for lengthy investigative cases are changes in attorney, changes (God forbid) in the investigative accountant, illness of one or more of the parties involved, vacation for one or more of the parties involved, replacement of the trial judge with another judge, etc.

APPENDIX B

SOURCES FOR COMPARATIVE INFORMATION

There are a multitude of sources from which one can obtain information regarding what to expect for a particular industry, what is normal, what the percentage ranges are, etc. The sources one chooses is up to the imagination of the practitioner. One obvious source that is often overlooked is your own client base. That is, talk to people you know, typically clients, that are familiar with the type of business you are investigating, and find out what they know about the business. For example, you may have clients, whether they be regular corporate clients or 1040 clients, who understand specific types of businesses in terms of what the gross profits are, where money can be skimmed, and where to find other information. Common sources of information for industry standards and comparisons include:

For industry in general	• Robert Morris Associates *Annual Statement Studies.*
	• Dun & Bradstreet *Ratio Analyses and Statistical Analyses.*
	• *U.S. Industrial Outlook,* published each year by the Department of Commerce
For medical practices	• American Medical Association's "Socioeconomic Characteristics of Medical Practice" (formerly, "Profile of Medical Practice").
	• various issues of *Medical Economics.*
For dental practices	• American Dental Association's "Survey of Dental Practice."
	• Bud Schulman's "Dental Finance Newsletter."
For general information	• various publications of the U.S. Department of Commerce and the Census Bureau.
For taxes	• The usual tax services and special tax books or services relating to pertinent areas.

When investigating a franchise operation, obtain selected information directly from franchise corporate headquarters. Usually, without too much effort, you should be able to obtain information relating to the expected volume of the typical franchise, gross profit percentages, and other expense relationships. Also, you should be able to obtain estimates of the expenditures necessary to establish a franchise and, perhaps, what it cost to establish a franchise last year or a few years ago — approximating the time that the business which you are investigating was established and/or the critical date. This, of course, could help you to appreciate the financial wherewithal necessary at the time that the franchise was purchased or established. Certainly, knowing directly from corporate or regional headquarters that a fast food franchise operation should be doing a gross profit of 68%, when the business you are investigating is showing 63%, immediately keys you in to the possibility, if not the likelihood, that something is wrong.

APPENDIX C

SAMPLE ENGAGEMENT LETTER

_____
(Date)

_____
_____
_____
_____

Re: Investigation of _____

_____

Dear _____ :

You have requested that we investigate _____, and
render an opinion as to the income of _____, and the
personal net worth of _____, as at _____.

Before preparing our opinion we wish to outline our understanding of the terms
of our engagement and the approach we will follow in performing the above
services.

We understand that you require this opinion for the purposes of the alimony and
support and equitable distribution issues relating to your pending divorce action.

Our approach will likely include:

a. A review and analysis of the financial activity of _____.
b. A review and analysis of the personal financial activity of _____.
c. Discussions and correspondence with management (to the extent we are given
   access) and other professional advisors to augment our knowledge of the
   operations of _____.
d. A review of relevant published market data and other public information
   available to us. We will describe any such information that we consider important in our report. Our report will not include any other market or similar
   surveys and our assessment will therefore provide only a general indication of
   the past performance and future prospects of _____.

e. Presentation to you of our preliminary findings following the completion of our study, including at that time an explanation of our approach and reasons for our conclusions.

f. Preparation and delivery of our final report thereafter.

Our final report is not intended for general circulation or publication, nor is it to be reproduced or used for any purpose other than that outlined above, without our prior written permission in each specific instance. We will not assume any responsibility or liability for losses occasioned to you or to other parties as a result of the circulation, publication, reproduction, or use of our report contrary to the provisions of this paragraph. The validity of our report is predicated on the extent to which full, honest, and complete disclosure is made by all parties.

In completing this engagement we will necessarily rely on information and material supplied by you. Therefore, in order for us to render a report, we require that you confirm in writing (by your signature to this letter) that you have no information or knowledge of any facts or material which would reasonably be expected to affect our conclusions except as you have disclosed to us.

It is agreed that you will pay us a retainer of _____, and that our fee will be based upon services rendered at the hourly rate of _____ per hour for the services of _____ and _____ to _____ per hour for the services of our staff, together with actual costs (telephone calls are chargeable time). We anticipate that once we have made reasonable progress in this matter, we will be in a position to confer with you to discuss the estimated total fee, exclusive of court testimony or deposition. The rate for court testimony or deposition is _____ per hour. It is further agreed that as the retainer is consumed, we will bill you for additional advance sums, and that the continuation of our services is contingent upon prompt payment of our billings. Invoices for services, which will be presented monthly, will be paid within 20 days from the invoice date.

For services rendered after _____, the above stated fees will increase as follows: for _____ to _____ per hour, for staff to between _____ and _____ per hour, for testimony or deposition to _____ per hour. Each _____ thereafter, these fees will increase approximately _____%.

It is further agreed that, if any of the above mentioned fees are assessed and paid by your spouse, you will receive a credit in that amount.

Please sign and return the enclosed copy of this letter.

Very truly yours,

ROSENBERG, FREUNDLICH, LEVINE,
KOPP & TRUGLIO, P.A.

Kalman A. Barson, CPA

I, _____, hereby agree to the above terms.

_____   _____
            Signature   Date

APPENDIX D

SAMPLE RECORDS DISCOVERY LETTER

_____
(Date)

_____
_____
_____
_____

Dear _____ :

As to _____, please have the following items available for our inspection or our files (where "copies" are requested). Unless otherwise indicated, the records requested are for the period _____.

1. Copies of any financial statements prepared internally or externally for any reason.
2. Copies of Federal and State income tax returns.
3. All books of original entry, including general ledgers, disbursements, receipts, sales, purchase and payroll journals.
4. Copies of any buy-sell agreements and employment contracts.
5. Copies of accountant's year-end worksheets, including journal entries.
6. All cancelled checks, checkbook stubs and bank statements.
7. All payroll records, including payroll returns.
8. All purchase and expense invoices, paid bills, and charge slips.
9. Appointment diaries.
10. Copies of year-end aged schedules of Accounts Receivable and Accounts Payable.
11. All sales invoices.
12. All inventory records.
13. Schedule of equipment (fixed assets), including motor vehicles.
14. Corporate and Director's book(s).
15. Stock register book(s) (since inception).
16. All insurance policies.
17. Copies of any revenue agent's reports.
18. Copies of any pension, profit sharing, and other employee benefit plans and the related records, statements, and transaction information.

Regarding your personal financial items, please have the following available for our inspection or our files (where "copies" are requested.) Unless otherwise indicated, the records requested are for the period _____.

1. Copies of any financial statements, whether prepared by you or someone else.
2. Copies of personal Federal and State income tax returns.
3. Copies of savings passbooks, statements, and other indicia of savings.
4. Stock brokerage monthly transaction sheets.
5. Cancelled checks and bank statements.
6. Schedule of tax free securities.
7. Personal insurance policies.
8. Copies of automobile, boat, or plane registrations owned individually.
9. Copies of any revenue agent's reports.

The above list may not be complete. Additional items may be requested as our inspection progresses.

Very truly yours,

Kalman A. Barson, CPA

APPENDIX E

SAMPLE FEE DEDUCTIBILITY LETTER

_____
(Date)

_____
_____
_____
_____

Dear _____ :

The following is relevant to the tax deductibility of the fees that you paid to our firm in 19___ .

It is our opinion that $_____ (or _____%) of these fees are deductible under Internal Revenue Code Section 212 as being for ordinary and necessary expenses in connection with the collection or production of income and determination and planning as to income taxation. Furthermore, it is our opinion that the nature of the work performed for you — including tax return preparation and amendment, tax planning and consultation, investigation of the income wherewithal and magnitude of compensation to _____, and the various other phases of our services detailed below — justifies and substantiates that the fees paid to our firm are tax deductible in the amount stated above. These services include:

- Assistance to (attorney) in matters of tax consequence.
- Investigation of _____ Company as to _____ 's compensation.
- Analysis of _____ 's banking records to determine his or her income and wherewithal.
- Attendance in court and conferences relevant to all issues herein.
- Conferences and correspondence with you and (attorney) relevant to all issues herein.
- Tax research on various issues relevant to court proceedings, including _____ .
- Preparation of report in this matter.
- Preparation of addendum to report in this matter.
- Analysis and review of various financial data submitted.

- Review and analysis of the personal tax returns of _____ for 19___ through 19___.
- Review and analysis of the tax returns and financial statements of _____ Company for 19___ through 19___.
- Tax research relevant to concerns of unreported income.
- Review of insurance maintained by _____ Company.
- Review of data relevant to retirement plan of _____ Company.
- Tax planning and consultation for 19___.
- Tax planning and consultation for 19___.
- Preparation of 19___ federal and state income tax returns.

I'll be in touch with you shortly to _____. In the meantime, if you have any questions, as always, please call.

Very truly yours,

Kalman A. Barson, CPA

APPENDIX F

WORK PROGRAMS

The work done in the investigative field, though not as routine as more common accounting work, can lend itself to using a work program. I find the work programs described and illustrated herein to be useful under certain circumstances. Frankly, many cases don't lend themselves to the ready use of a work program inasmuch as there are numerous questions, unknowns, etc. Also, the budgeted and actual time columns are not often easily used. It is difficult to project a budgeted time for a certain phase of the work when dealing with a nonrecurring client; and you do not have the luxury of spending a day in advance with the client, going over a work program and determining a timeframe.

The actual time elements in this type of work is a problem in that many jobs run into each other. Sometimes you will abruptly disrupt one phase of your work because you've come across something else that requires your immediate attention. Also, many jobs of this nature put you under great time pressure, and the preparation of a work program, if done properly, is going to take several hours, and additional time to maintain the work program. Therefore, there will be many times when you will not have the ability to utilize the luxury of a work program, even though it would be desirable from a theoretical accounting point of view.

We have presented herein three work programs. The nature of the work lends itself to classification into a few categories, which we have determined can well be put into these three programs. The first one will be for the preliminary, continuous type of work, the post fieldwork, and the report. These phases of the work are common to any of the assignments that you get in the investigative area and, therefore, even though part of it is at the beginning and part of it at the end of our work, it lends itself to being placed in one document — Work Program A.

Next, Work Program B for the business phase of your work. Use a separate work program for each business investigated; often there are multiple businesses and related corporations. It is good practice to maintain a separate work program for each.

Finally, Work Program C for the personal investigation phase of your work. This includes looking into the financial and banking records of the individuals involved.

The freewheeling nature of some of the work that we have to do in the investigative area mandates a certain degree of flexibility in how these work programs are handled. They should not be construed in any way to have the rigidity of the by-the-book requirements of a typical audit program.

Unlike the standard audit or work program types with which readers are probably familiar, the work programs herein do not go into any great depth as to what steps are expected to be performed. For instance, in a typical audit program, the steps in the cash function are extremely detailed and voluminous. Included are steps indicating that for each bank account you are to test check two months of reconciliations, look at 30 checks each month for endorsement and signature, compare to bank confirmations, etc. These steps can run on for a few pages — just for the cash function. The intent and concept here is that the user is expected to understand what's involved in this type of work, and be able to, from a few key words, perform whatever steps are necessary. Furthermore, audit style is not usually applicable in this work.

APPENDIX G

INITIAL AND WRAP-UP WORK PROGRAM

DESCRIPTION	N/A	BUDGETED TIME	ACTUAL TIME	DONE BY
1. Obtain documentation from attorney and/or client, such as interrogatories, tax returns, financial statements, etc.				
2. Set up folder and organize into file sections to include: interrogatories, workpapers, business tax returns and financial statements, personal tax returns and supporting data, correspondence files, workpaper file for each business investigated, report, agreements, appraisals, etc.				
3. Review documentation; make notes of questions to be raised.				
4. Conference with wife, husband, dissident parties − whatever.				
5. Discuss fees and payment arrangements with client.				
6. Conference with attorney(s).				
7. Contact the other side's representative(s) by phone to arrange for initial investigative work. Send follow-up confirmation letter.				
8. Send records discovery letter requesting the specific information to be reviewed.				
9. Especially where cooperation is not readily forthcoming, document correspondence and telephone calls.				
10. Obtain copies of everything and anything that appears to be important.				

DESCRIPTION	N/A	BUDGETED TIME	ACTUAL TIME	DONE BY
11. Compare findings to interrogatories. Follow up discrepancies.				
WRAP-UP				
12. Be sure work is adequately documented — assume going to testify in court.				
13. Prepare report. Keep it balanced and even-handed.				
14. In report, as to personal net worth, don't overlook the add-back of business loans receivable and subtraction of business loans payable.				
15. Other steps.				

APPENDIX H

BUSINESS WORK PROGRAM

DESCRIPTION	N/A	BUDGETED TIME	ACTUAL TIME	DONE BY
1. Organize approach and know which businesses need to be reviewed.				
2. Be sure you have at least three years of business records available for inspection.				
3. Do preliminary review of tax returns and financial statements for areas of potential discovery and investigation.				
4. Review the general ledger for insight.				
5. Compare financial statements to general ledger to tax returns				
6. Physical inspection of operation.				
BALANCE SHEET				
7. Review cash accounts. Schedule all accounts, including bank and account numbers and type of account. Review checks for endorsements.				
8. Review petty cash documentation.				
9. Schedule marketable securities and other cash equivalents. Determine current fair market value. Segregate P and L effect of marketable security transactions from operation.				
10. Review accounts receivable — aging, magnitude of individual customers, and write-offs.				

DESCRIPTION	N/A	BUDGETED TIME	ACTUAL TIME	DONE BY
11. Bad debt reserve — analyze for reasonableness.				
12. Inventory — reasonableness, adequacy, and basis for valuation. Obtain copies of year end (and interim if available) inventory schedules.				
13. Prepaid expenses — properly reflected?				
14. Loans and exchanges — watch for any washing of funds, related parties, etc.				
15. Officer loans — trace all sources of monies in and all dispositions of monies out. Inspect endorsements on checks.				
16. Fixed assets — review depreciation methods, accumulated depreciation and current carrying value, and contents of fixed asset account. Verify who uses which vehicles, and the business connection of these people. Obtain schedules of all fixed asset accounts — reconcile and analyze.				
17. Patents and other intangibles — obtain as much supporting documentation as possible.				
18. Security deposits and other assets.				
19. Accounts payable — inspect aging and data as to key suppliers.				
20. Loans payable — determine disposition of funds, interest rates, and maturity dates.				
21. Payroll taxes payable.				
22. Sales taxes payable.				
23. Equity — thoroughly review any changes in the past several years.				
24. Dividends — schedule and ascertain in proportion to stock holdings.				

DESCRIPTION	N/A	BUDGETED TIME	ACTUAL TIME	DONE BY
25. Stock record and minutes books — review, analyze and schedule as appropriate.				
26. Sales — analyze and understand extent of major customers and transactions with related companies. Does it appear all sales are reported.				
27. Sales returns and allowances — analyze for unusual transactions.				
28. Cost of goods sold — test for unusual postings and for reasonableness.				
29. Officer's salary — detailed schedule. Reconcile to personal finances analysis.				
30. Other payroll. Review for familiar names; tie W-2's.				
31. Rent — watch for related party situations.				
32. Repairs and maintenance — watch for personal and capitalizable.				
33. Insurance–inspect policies; watch for values in excess of book.				
34. Travel and entertainment — documentation; economic income.				
35. Automobile expenses.				
36. Telephone expense.				
37. Office supplies.				
38. Dues and subscriptions.				
39. Utilities expense.				
40. Professional Fees — detailed analysis.				
41. Payroll Taxes — reasonable?				
42. Tax expense — other.				
43. Officer's life insurance expense — inspect.				
44. Employee benefits.				

DESCRIPTION	N/A	BUDGETED TIME	ACTUAL TIME	DONE BY
45. Interest expense – reconcile to loans.				
46. Fines and penalties.				
47. Bad debts.				
48. Miscellaneous expenses – watch for major items.				
49. Depreciation – analyze supporting worksheets and methods used.				
50. Retirement plans – types of plans and amount of allocations.				
51. General journal and journal entries – overview.				
52. Cash checks – investigate for documentation and endorsements.				
53. Review governmental reports, if any. Tie key items to books and records, financial statements, tax returns, etc.				
54. Cash disbursements journal – overview for standout items.				
55. Cash receipts journal – overview for standout items.				
56. Purchase journal – overview for standout items.				
57. Review all papers and questions raised. Make sure as much is answered as possible.				
58. Other steps.				

APPENDIX I

PERSONAL FINANCES WORK PROGRAM

DESCRIPTION	N/A	BUDGETED TIME	ACTUAL TIME	DONE BY
1. Review all personal bank records–savings and checking.				
2. Review all personal brokerage accounts and other indicia of savings.				
3. Correlate deposits into personal accounts (banks, brokerage, etc.) with known income sources.				
4. 1040's – review in depth.				
5. Determine if expenses from personal accounts approximate lifestyle.				
6. Reconstruct standard of living to determine if reported income can account for same.				
7. Compare state income tax returns to federal income tax returns for any variances.				
8. Determine if collections (coins, stamps, etc.) exist.				
9. Other steps.				

APPENDIX J

SAMPLE REPORTS

The following five sample reports are presented to illustrate the type of work, and work product, you can expect to experience in this segment of accounting service. There are certainly many other types of reports that can be rendered as a result of investigative accounting — more reports than could possibly be illustrated herein.

The following sample reports are from five different, unrelated cases. The numbers and details are largely as originally presented to the judges, attorneys, or clients, with, for the most part, limited changes made to protect confidentiality.

Mr./Ms. Attorney

Re: Spouse vs Spouse

Dear Attorney:

Detailed herein are the alimony necessary for Mrs. Spouse (and her three minor children) to maintain their budgeted lifestyle (utilizing four alternative upfront cash distributions), the consequences of same, and information relevant to the proposed sale of the marital residence. The following assumptions are integral factors in this analysis:

1. Mrs. Spouse will continue to be employed, and earn approximately $16,500 in 1983.
2. Mr. Spouse will pay for the home mortgage (or equivalent).
3. Head of household tax status for Mrs. Spouse and one of the three children as her dependent.
4. An 8% return on the upfront cash distribution, and no invasion of principal.
5. Additional upfront cash to pay for legal and expert fees — so as not to reduce the earning capacity of Item 4 above.
6. An annual budget of $43,620 (as detailed herein) — which reflects somewhat diminished budget requirements due to Mr. Spouse's limited degree of shared custody (and the resultant shared expenses).
7. "Alimony" will be unallocated — fully taxable to Mrs. Spouse and fully deductible by Mr. Spouse.
8. No provision was made to allow Mrs. Spouse to provide herself with an annual IRA contribution.
9. No provision was made for inflation (a cost of living adjustment).
10. Mrs. Spouse will invest available funds only in secure, liquid vehicles.

It is interesting to note that, with Mrs. Spouse's budget needs, and with her three sources of income being taxable, she will be in a marginal (federal plus state) tax bracket of 46% — considerably higher than that of Mr. Spouse, who has the ability and wherewithal to shelter a substantial portion of his income. Therefore, consideration should be given to designating some portion of the payments to Mrs. Spouse as child support. This would reduce her tax burden, thereby enabling Mr. Spouse to make lesser alimony/support payments, while still meeting Mrs. Spouse's budget requirements. This evening out of the tax brackets would save Mr. Spouse money by reducing the combined tax burden.

ALTERNATIVE ALIMONY PAYMENTS FOR MRS. SPOUSE

	ASSUMING AN UP-FRONT CASH DISTRIBUTION OF			
	$80,000	$120,000	$150,000	$200,000
Mrs. Spouse's salary	$16,500	$16,500	$16,500	$16,500
Interest on distribution at 8%	6,400	9,600	12,000	16,000
ALIMONY REQUIREMENTS	40,620	37,420	35,020	31,020
TOTAL – GROSS – BEFORE TAXES	63,520	63,520	63,520	63,520
TAXES AND OTHER WITHHOLDINGS:				
Federal income tax	17,295	17,295	17,295	17,295
New Jersey income tax	1,553	1,553	1,553	1,553
FICA tax	1,106	1,106	1,106	1,106
Other payroll withholdings	906	906	906	906
Dependent care credit	(960)	(960)	(960)	(960)
NET TAX BURDEN	19,900	19,900	19,900	19,900
NET – AFTER TAXES = BUDGET	$43,620	$43,620	$43,620	$43,620
MARGINAL COMBINED INCOME TAX BRACKET	46%	46%	46%	46%
ALIMONY REQUIREMENTS – AS ABOVE:				
Annual	$40,620	$37,420	$35,020	$31,020
Monthly	3,385	3,118	2,918	2,585
Weekly	781	720	673	597

As a rough example, the alimony of $40,620 (for the $80,000 lump sum alternative) could be restructured to be $15,000 alimony and $15,000 child support — reducing Mr. Spouse's (before tax) outlay by $10,620. Yet, because of the nontaxability of the child support to Mrs. Spouse, her net (after tax) proceeds from such would actually increase by over one thousand dollars — even though she would be receiving $10,620 less. Her marginal (federal plus state) tax bracket in this scenario would be 36%.

Although the above plan offers some worthwhile alternatives and deserves serious consideration, Mrs. Spouse must be adequately protected from reductions in the payments arising from the maturity of each child. Consideration must be given as to her needs once the children reach majority, when the $30,000 combined annual payments (in the above scenario) drop to $15,000.

As to the sale of the marital residence, inasmuch as it is jointly owned, the sale presents tax consequences to both Mr. and Mrs. Spouse, regardless of whether the residence is sold prior to or after the divorce. Presuming that the house has been held for longer than one year, they will each sustain a capital gain equal to one-half of the total gain. Where a sale of a principal residence is followed or preceded within a period of 24 months after or before that sale by the purchase or construction of a replacement principal residence, any gain is recognized only so far as the adjusted sales price of the old residence exceeds the cost of the new one. That is, regardless of the existence of any mortgages, if the new house costs more than the sale price (her share) of the old house, there is no gain to be immediately recognized — any gain is deferred. These rules are mandatory — there is no option in terms of choosing between reporting a gain or postponing it.

The following illustrates the calculation of the gain based on the facts as stated in your letter. We are utilizing a sales price of $365,000 — the midpoint of your proposed sales price range.

Half of the adjusted sales price	$182,500
Less cost of new residence	160,000
Gain to be recognized	$ 22,500
One-half of sales price	$182,500
Less half the cost of the old residence	93,500
Share of gain	89,000
Less gain to be recognized (above)	22,500
Deferred gain	66,500
Cost of new residence	160,000
Less deferred gain (above)	66,500
Adjusted basis of new residence	$ 93,500

The above excludes the impact of any legal or other closing costs and realty commissions. These items either increase the basis or reduce the sales price and, therefore, reduce the gain.

It should be pointed out that, in addition to the general deferral provisions discussed above, upon reaching age 55, Mrs. Spouse may avail herself of the once-in-a-lifetime exclusion of up to $125,000 of gain attributable to the sale of a personal residence. Hence, some or all of the gain upon the sale of Mrs. Spouse's new residence, despite the reduced basis of $93,500, may permanently escape taxation.

As to Mrs. Spouse buying a house for $160,000 with the options that she has of either obtaining a mortgage or paying for the house outright, the answer is not the simplest in that it is not always a straight financial or economic decision. What is the expected return on invested funds that are not used towards the purchase of the house? As an example, current money market rates are only around 8 or 8-1/2%. There are fairly secure corporate bonds available in the 10 to 12% area. There are less secure corporate bonds available in the 15 and higher percent return area. There are also municipals of varying returns in the current market, from as low as 5% to as high as 10 or 12%. In general, it may not be advisable to invest in medium or long term bonds, whether they be corporate or municipals, because of the chance that interest rates will turn upwards again within the next couple of years.

We offer below various alternatives using 12% and 13% as mortgage rates (currently reasonable available rates) and payout terms of 20, 25, and 30 years. We also assume a 20% downpayment ($32,000) with the balance ($128,000) in the form of a mortgage. The monthly interest and principal amortization on such a mortgage would be as follows:

NO. OF YEARS	12%	13%
20	$1,409	$1,500
25	1,348	1,456
30	1,317	1,416

Not expressed above, but often a significant factor, is that Mrs. Spouse should expect perhaps three points up front (3% of $128,000 being $3,840) and legal and other closing fees in the vicinity of $1,000 — most of these expenses she wouldn't have if there were no mortgage. Of course, regardless of the existence of a mortgage or not, there will be approximately $300 a month of real estate taxes.

To the extent that one takes a mortgage, yet remains fairly liquid in case there is a cash flow crunch, one can always dip into the monetary reserve that was retained by the use of a mortgage. The funds left over can and should be invested wisely. It is anticipated that, unless a fair amount of risk is willing to be assumed, the return on the invested funds will be less than the interest rate charged on the mortgage. It is likely that the spread will be about four points, based on current market rates. This, by itself, suggests that the wisest move is to buy the house outright and assume no mortgage. However, this would mean the commitment of a very large sum of money — and there is some value to having liquid and ready assets available. Of course, a house does generally represent a fairly liquid asset to the extent that it can be mortgaged, usually within a four week period.

A final factor concerning the issue of purchasing a house outright vs. obtaining a mortgage is basically a noneconomic one; that is, a peace of mind that comes with having the fewest number of fixed monthly payments and obligations. If having a hefty mortgage would cause Mrs. Spouse to lose sleep, notwithstanding the financial and economic justification of such, then certainly it would be worth it for her, in her financial situation, not to have the burden of a mortgage.

HEALING VS HEALING

REPORT OF FINDINGS

TABLE OF CONTENTS

Learned Counsel
Attorney & Lawyer P.A.

Re: Healing vs Healing

Dear Ms. Counsel:

On behalf of Mrs. Rebecca Healing, we reviewed the records of The Healing Group, P.A., a medical practice owned and operated by her former husband. We also reviewed the checkbook of the real estate partnership known as Healing & Recovery.

We prepared and submit herein reconstructed operating results of The Healing Group P.A. for the fifteen month period ended June 30, 1983. Our Introductory comments on Pages 3 and 4 must be included in any consideration of Dr. Healing's total financial picture.

This report should not be considered as an audit in accordance with generally accepted accounting principles, but an investigatory review prepared for the purpose of determining Dr. Healing's income.

If we can be of further service, please call.

Very Truly Yours,

Kalman A. Barson, CPA
Member of the Firm

HEALING VS HEALING

SUMMARY OF FINDINGS

(Numbers rounded to nearest thousand)

The sources of income for Dr. Healing and his approximate annual income therefrom, are as follows:

The Healing Group	$195,000
Healing & Recovery	5,000
Laboratory Services Group	?
Interest, dividends, and other	?
ANNUAL INCOME (IN EXCESS OF)	$200,000

HEALING VS HEALING

INTRODUCTORY COMMENTS

We were engaged to determine the income of Dr. Healing. To that end, our review was to include access to all books and records of ventures in which Dr. Healing has a material interest, and also his 1982 personal income tax return. These ventures are The Healing Group, P.A., the partnership known as Healing & Recovery, and the Laboratory Services Group.

The Healing Group, P.A. is the main source of income for Dr. Healing. We were given access to certain of its books and records. Refer to Notes, especially Numbers 4, 5, 7, 10, 11, 14, and 15. We were refused access to the cash receipts journals and accounts receivable cards. These latter items are essential to verifying the accuracy of recorded income. Inasmuch as we could not so verify income, we can express no opinion as to its accuracy as recorded, except to refer to our notes explaining the problems, errors, and misrepresentations we found with the recorded expenses.

Healing & Recovery owns the medical building in which The Healing Group (besides the Laboratory Services Group and others) operates. We were able to review its checkbook and 1982 information return. Inasmuch as 1982 was the first year of rental operations for this partnership, an accurate determination of the income it yields to Dr. Healing is difficult. Based on 1982, it appears that, before depreciation (which, in a real estate venture is a tax benefit, not an actual economic expense), Dr. Healing may realize a positive cash flow of approximately $5,000 per year.

We were given a mutilated copy of what was allegedly Dr. Healing's 1982 personal income tax return. This copy had been rendered almost totally useless by the obliteration of much of the significant information.

As to the Laboratory Services Group, we were advised by Dr. Healing that he has no interest in same, and, therefore, there would be no records for us to review. Our presence in his office, and our review of the records of the partnership Healing & Recovery, indicated to us that we were not told the truth and that information that should have been available to us was intentionally withheld. Conversation among the staff in Dr. Healing's office included reference to the Lab Group with its telephone number being answered in the Doctor's office. Most convincing, however, was the finding of two checks, payable to the Laboratory from the partnership, apparently to set up a checking account for the Laboratory. Since the partnership is one-third owned by Dr. Healing, it is obvious that, contrary to what we were advised, he did have an interest in the Lab Group.

There was a significant problem in getting a reasonable degree of cooperation, and we were still denied access to much information and records documentation. As perhaps an indication of the extent of the problems, we were shown two inadequate "bills" to support payments to "Head Industries" (see Notes 8 and 9). While these "bills" could not prove the business relationship of the expense, it should be noted that the correct name is "Head Meats." It appears that a conscious effort was made to avoid having anything so flagrantly questionable being highlighted in the disbursements journal by misrepresenting the name.

THE HEALING GROUP, P.A.
RECONSTRUCTED STATEMENT OF INCOME (UNAUDITED)
FOR FIFTEEN MONTHS ENDED JUNE 30, 1983

	PER BOOKS AND RECORDS				
	PER FORM 1120 YEAR ENDED 9/30/82	LESS SIX MONTHS ENDED 3/31/82	SIX MONTHS ENDED 9/30/82	NINE MONTHS ENDED 6/30/83	FIFTEEN MONTHS ENDED 6/30/83
INCOME					
Income from fees – Note 2	$375,845	$172,603	$203,242	$349,341	$552,583
Interest income	59	30	29	30	59
TOTAL INCOME	375,904	172,633	203,271	349,371	552,642
EXPENSES					
Other salaries–Note 3	102,620	63,045	39,575	82,880	122,455
Consulting fees – Note 4	12,739	—	12,739	9,000	21,739
Medical supplies – Note 5	31,537	15,769	15,768	17,596	33,364
Rent	20,553	7,694	12,859	23,146	36,005
Utilities – Note 6	4,184	2,286	1,898	3,133	5,031
Office maintenance – Note 7	2,741	1,088	1,653	4,086	5,739
Office supplies – Note 8	6,078	2,078	4,000	5,488	9,488
Office expense – Note 9	17,251	4,940	12,311	14,910	27,221
Collection expense	—	—	—	3,117	3,117
Telephone – Note 6	8,322	3,838	4,484	6,103	10,587
Automobile – Note 10	6,633	1,550	5,083	4,563	9,646
Insurance – Note 11	29,514	14,757	14,757	35,638	50,395
Health and Welfare – Note 12	969	434	535	1,482	2,017
Medical licenses and dues	2,531	1,665	866	2,650	3,516
Medical books and journals	627	16	611	729	1,340
Medical conventions and seminars – Note 13	461	400	61	4,228	4,289
Legal – Note 14	4,126	1,600	2,526	750	3,276
Accounting – Note 14	3,250	2,000	1,250	750	2,000
Entertainment and gifts – Note 15	10,043	5,191	4,852	11,434	16,286
Interest	3,396	1,141	2,255	3,614	5,869
Payroll taxes – Note 16	7,905	3,953	3,952	10,168	14,120
Other taxes	602	602	—	178	178
Loss due to abandonment of leasehold improvements – Note 17	1,643	821	822	—	822
Depreciation – note 18	11,727	5,863	5,864	8,482	14,346
Amortization of leasehold improvements	444	222	222	695	917
TOTAL EXPENSES	289,896	140,953	148,943	254,820	403,763
NET INCOME AND DR. HEALING'S SALARY	$ 86,008	$ 31,680	$ 54,328	$ 94,551	$148,879

	ADJUSTMENTS			ADJUSTED	
	SIX MONTHS ENDED 9/30/82	NINE MONTHS ENDED 6/30/83	FIFTEEN MONTHS ENDED 6/30/83	FIFTEEN MONTHS ENDED 6/30/83	ANNUALIZED ADJUSTED
	$ 310	$ 891	$ 1,201	$553,784	$443,027
	—	—	—	59	47
	310	891	1,201	553,843	443,074
	—	(1,400)	(1,400)	121,055	96,844
	(12,739)	(9,000)	(21,739)	—	—
	(576)	(2,288)	(2,864)	30,500	24,400
	—	—	—	36,005	28,804
	—	(443)	(443)	4,588	3,670
	—	(1,240)	(1,240)	4,499	3,599
	(2,553)	(874)	(3,427)	6,061	4,849
	(7,737)	(12,518)	(20,255)	6,966	5,573
	—	—	—	3,117	2,494
	—	(984)	(984)	9,603	7,682
	(3,985)	(3,388)	(7,373)	2,273	1,818
	(4,531)	(2,605)	(7,136)	43,259	34,607
	(300)	(847)	(1,147)	870	696
	—	—	—	3,516	2,813
	—	—	—	1,340	1,072
	—	(2,071)	(2,071)	2,218	1,774
	(2,500)	—	(2,500)	776	621
	(188)	(112)	(300)	1,700	1,360
	(3,480)	(9,947)	(13,427)	2,859	2,287
	—	—	—	5,869	4,695
	(965)	(3,049)	(4,014)	10,106	8,085
	—	—	—	178	142
	(822)	—	(822)	—	—
	(1,873)	(399)	(2,272)	12,074	9,659
	(66)	—	(66)	851	681
	(42,315)	(51,165)	(93,480)	310,283	248,225
	$ 42,625	$ 52,056	$ 94,681	$243,560	$194,849

THE HEALING GROUP, P.A

NOTES TO RECONSTRUCTED STATEMENT OF INCOME

FOR THE FIFTEEN MONTHS ENDED JUNE 30, 1983

NOTE 1.   The income statement for the six months ended September 30, 1982 was reconstructed by reviewing the summaries of cash receipts and disbursements of the practice. Where it was not practical to determine a reasonably precise allocation between periods, it was assumed that 50% of the expenses occurred in each 6 month period.

NOTE 2.   Income from fees — we reclassified nine checks recorded as patient reimbursements. The check stubs indicated four were for personal dental bills, one for glasses, one to a psychologist, and three to cut grass.

NOTE 3.   Other salaries — This adjustment represents eight checks for $175 to Dr. Healing's minor children classified as payroll. These checks had no taxes withheld from them, and appear to have been for personal expenses.

NOTE 4.   Consulting fees — We removed payments to Dr. Emily Holistic, who was employed by The Healing Group until February 1982. We were not permitted to review her employment agreement. It appears that these payments were in the nature of a nondeductible buy-out, rather than deductible compensation.

NOTE 5.   Medical supplies — We reclassified the following five checks:

PAYEE	DESCRIPTION	AMOUNT
Hands-On Equipment Co.	P-T Equipment (Capitalized)	$1,000
The Electronic Supply House	Video Cassette (Capitalized)	788
Lola's	No bill	500
All City	Auto Insurance	286
CYA Insurance Co.	Building Insurance	290
TOTAL		$2,864

NOTE 6.   Utilities and telephone — Dr. Healing ceased paying his home telephone and utility bills through his personal account in September 1982. At that time, he moved into a new residence and The Healing Group began paying two telephone and utility bills. We were given access only to one of the monthly bills — the practice's.

NOTE 7.   Office maintenance — We adjusted eleven items recorded as office maintenance; seven of these were marked oil. They all occurred after September 1982. No bills were made available to us and it appears that these were the personal heating bills for Dr. Healing. The four remaining items included a $200 check to his son, and three small checks for lawn maintenance.

NOTE 8.   Office supplies — We reclassified sixteen items: three checks to Graduate University for Dr. Healing's son, an unexplained $150 check to his (new) wife, a check to cash for $350, a check to Head Industries for meat, $450 to Lola's marked as personal on the stub, $209 to the Rack, marked clothes, $1,455 to Caterer's Delight for a party, and various smaller checks.

NOTE 9.   Office expense — Over 100 checks, covering the following items were reclassified:

PAYEE	DESCRIPTION	NUMBER OF CHECKS	TOTAL AMOUNT
Marmaduke Healing	Doctor's Son	14	$ 1,047
Oscar Healing	Doctor's Son	10	420
Isaac Jones	Doctor's Son's friend	12	305
Zelda Healing	Doctor's (new) wife	8	1,287
Rising-Star Healing	Doctor's daughter	2	108
Cash	Other	2	1,678
Cash	Appraisal of diamonds	3	1,225
Cash	Other	7	2,298
Marina del Doc	Repair son's boat	4	345
Head Industries	Doctor's meat market	12	777
Various capitalized items	Office furniture	12	5,928
All-Star Sports Camp	for Rising-Star	1	95
Maintenance Co.	Landscaping	1	416
EAB	Architect	1	658
Miscellaneous	Many checks	34	3,668
TOTAL			$20,255

NOTE 10.   Automobile — The doctor owns and drives a Mercedes. It is three years old and has 63,000 miles on it. The doctor advised us that he averages four trips to the local hospital each day. Each round trip is less than one mile. He also goes, one day per week, to Our Lady of Speedy Healing Hospital, a distance of 44 miles. On 75% of Saturday mornings, he drives to seminars, averaging 64 miles round trip.

DESCRIPTION	TOTAL
To local hospital: 4 trips @ 1 mile @ 5 days per week	20
To OLSHH: 1 trip @ 44 miles	44
To Seminars: 3/4 trips @ 64	48
Total business mileage per week	112
Number of weeks	50
Total Business miles per year	5,600
Divided by total annual mileage of	21,000
Percent of business use	26.7%

Some of the gas bills were signed by the doctor's wife, some bills were missing, and we did not have access to many bills. The doctor is paid $2,500, plus all gas and repairs for the use of his car. We subtracted the bills which were not for the doctor's car, and multiplied the remainder by 73.3%, to arrive at the personal portion of the automobile expenses.

NOTE 11. Insurance — We reclassified 20 checks totalling $7,136 as personal. In most cases, neither the policies nor the bills were available to us. Instead, we were obliged to use a brief schedule of policies. The items reclassified included the doctor's homeowner policy, his portion of disability and hospitalization policies, life insurance, automobile insurance, and a $500 check to Lola's for a party.

NOTE 12. Health and Welfare — We reclassified six checks for personal medical expenses of Dr. Healing.

NOTE 13. Medical Conventions and Seminars — The following two checks were reclassified:

PAYEE	DESCRIPTION	AMOUNT
Travel Agent Inc.	Super Bowl	$1,467
Roadside Motel	No explanation	604
TOTAL		$2,071

NOTE 14. Legal and Accounting — We were advised that no bills are submitted by the attorneys or the accountants. This highly unusual procedure hampered our review. However, we were able to determine the personal nature of the following items:

PAYEE	DESCRIPTION	AMOUNT
Advocacy Plus	Divorce Counsel	$1,500
EAB	Architect	1,300
TOTAL		$2,800

NOTE 15. Entertainment and gifts — No bills were made available to us for American Express and other credit cards. Furthermore, we were advised that the Doctor did not keep a diary. We reclassified as personal the following:

PAYEE	DESCRIPTION	NUMBER OF CHECKS	TOTAL
American Express	No supporting documents	15	$ 5,625
Bate & Takkel	Fishing trip	1	350
Quary-side	The dock for son's boat	1	82
Local Hospital Cafeteria and Coffee Shop	Dr. Healing's lunches and dinners	12	1,208
Dr. Healing	No description	1	297
The Eatery	Dr. Healing's lunches	6	61
Aristotle's Retreat	No description	1	650
Dr. Healing	No description	2	379
Burning Bush	Cigars and gifts	2	231
Last State Bank	Mastercharge	5	1,531
Bankamericard	No description	1	100
Visa	No description	1	244
Bate & Takkel	Fishing trips	4	1,280
Zelda Healing	Doctor's (new) wife	1	175
Various smaller checks			1,214
TOTAL			$13,427

NOTE 16. Payroll taxes — A check to the Internal Revenue Service, dated 1/17/83, for $1,622, was in payment of Dr. Healing's individual income taxes, yet was included in the payroll tax expense. In addition, Dr. Healing had no FICA withheld from his wages for the fifteen month period examined. Therefore, the "Company" paid and deducted $2,392 of personal FICA withholding tax on behalf of Dr. Healing.

NOTE 17. Loss on abandonment — This item was disregarded as being non-recurring and, therefore, not indicative of the ongoing medical practice.

NOTE 18. Depreciation — We adjusted depreciation to correct the improper depreciation method used by the medical practice. We also included depreciation on the expensed items that we capitalized.

ABBOTT VS COSTELLO

REPORT OF FINDINGS

TABLE OF CONTENTS

The Honorable Judge Decision

Re: Abbott vs Costello
Docket No. 1952

Dear Judge Decision:

On behalf of the Court, we evaluated the available financial records relevant to the "Becka" and "Emmy" properties in the above matter. The purpose of our evaluation and report was to determine the true cost of those properties so as to enable the Court to make a determination as to the parties' respective interests.

This report should not be considered as an audit in accordance with generally accepted accounting principles, but rather an investigatory evaluation prepared for the purposes as detailed above.

Respectfully submitted,

Kalman A. Barson, CPA

cc: Abbott attorney
     Costello attorney
     Abbott
     Costello

ABBOTT VS COSTELLO

GENERAL COMMENTS

A. We bring to the Court's attention, the question of the value, if any, accorded Mr. Costello in the agreement, for the loss of use of his funds. That is, is it a matter of concern here that the purchase money mortgage, involved in the acquisition of the Becka property, was payable in three years? Would Mr. Costello be entitled to offset, as an expense, the additional interest on the mortgage if it were payable in ten years? Or, is the percentage of Mr. Costello's share of profits in partial recognition of his expenses?

B. The Court must address itself to the situation that Mr. Costello, for several years, has occupied, as his personal residence, the home at 7-11 Dispute Road, Bridgewater, which is part of this dispute. Various expenses and capital improvements in this report pertain to that residence. Certainly, some portion of any improvements have increased the value of the house and, therefore, have inured to the benefit of both Mr. Abbott and Mr. Costello. However, an inescapable fact, and a very significant one, is that Mr. Costello has used that house as his personal residence. We leave it to the Court to determine what a fair rental should have been, a part of which Mr. Costello might have been entitled to as his share of profits — should there be an offset of some dollar amount for the personal occupancy of the property by Mr. Costello. Also, please refer to Comment C below.

C. Mr. Costello explained that in the late 1960's, the house at 7-11 Dispute Road was repaired so that it would be rentable, and that in fact the house was rented for some period of time — the exact amount of time unspecified. I inquired as to the rental income. Mr. Costello explained, and I present this to the Court for its consideration, that rental income was *not* subject to this agreement and, therefore, has not been reflected and the information not supplied. I suggest that the Court tend to the question of whether or not the agreement between Mr. Abbott and Mr. Costello would allow for any rental income to inure to the sole benefit of Mr. Costello, or whether the rental income should be a direct offset against expenses, or whether the rental income should be considered part of the profits and divided between Mr. Abbott and Mr. Costello.

D. We do not offer a conclusion as to the bottom line profits on the Becka property. Our schedule of costs lists considerable amounts that were not proven but are possible. We have also raised issues that only the Court can adequately answer. We feel it would be a relatively easy matter, once certain critical items, as set forth, are settled, to establish a true profit for the property. Other complicating factors include that certain of the expenses are directly attributible to the existing house, two lots have not yet been sold, and the value of the existing two lots and the house need to be determined. Such are matters for one expert in real estate valuation.

ABBOTT VS COSTELLO

BECKA PROPERTY

COSTS AND SALES PROCEEDS THROUGH DECEMBER 31, 1983

NOTE	COSTS			
	SUBMITTED BY COSTELLO	PROVEN AND ACCEPTED	NOT PROVEN – BUT POSSIBLE	NOT PERTINENT
Purchase of land	$ 98,000	$ 98,000	$	$
Interest on purchase money mortgage	8,460	8,460		
1. Mortgage – Bank of Sark –including interest	49,657			49,657
Real estate taxes	47,669	47,669		
Legal fees	4,837	4,837		
2. Engineering and other expert fees	3,532	3,029	503	
3. Architect	6,000		6,000	
4. Out of pocket expenses	1,100		1,100	
5. "Renovation" of existing house 1971–1974	23,138	3,411	18,063	1,664
Replacement of gutters	1,314	1,314		
6. Allowance for office, telephone, and secretarial	4,000		4,000	
7. Central air conditioning	3,500		3,500	
8. Income tax on profit at sale	12,218			12,218
TOTALS	$263,425	$166,720	$ 33,166	$ 63,539

9., 10. *Sales Proceeds*
9 Lots at $14,250 –
September, 1977 $128,250
Less 2 lots – "Louie" at
$14,250   28,500
"Adjusted" proceeds $ 99,750

ABBOTT VS COSTELLO
EMMY PROPERTY
COSTS AND SALES PROCEEDS THROUGH DECEMBER 31, 1983

	COSTS		
NOTE	SUBMITTED BY COSTELLO	PROVEN AND ACCEPTED	NOT PROVEN – BUT POSSIBLE
Purchase of land	$ 24,933	$ 24,933	$ —
Realtor commission	1,020	1,020	—
11. Engineering and legal	5,564	3,340	2,224
Real estate taxes	10,472	10,472	—
Various other expenses	424	424	—
4. Out of pocket expenses	1,100	—	1,100
Interest on mortgage	750	750	—
12. Landscaping and fill	1,343	—	1,343
TOTALS	$ 45,606	$ 40,939	$ 4,667

13. *Sales Proceeds*
     May, 1968 $ 16,997
     Condemnation – September 1979   18,500
          TOTAL PROCEEDS $ 35,497

ABBOTT VS COSTELLO

NOTES

1. Mortgage — Bank of Sark — including interest. Presented to me during my meeting at Mr. Costello's office, by himself and his accountant — was a copy of a mortgage instrument relevant to the Becka property. It was for $35,000 at 9% — $443.37 per month over a ten year period, starting November 1, 1974. The proceeds of this mortgage were used for the July 6, 1974 payment of the $24,000 balance on the acquisition of the Becka property. There remained $8,977.68 excess proceeds, which went directly to Costello. I have totally rejected this item, outright, as not being relevant. Specifically, to allow this would be a duplication of the cost of the property inasmuch as this latter mortgage, in part, was used to pay off an existing mortgage; in addition, almost $9,000 went directly to Mr. Costello. Similarly, the interest expense, which amounted to over $14,000, was not allowed.

2. Engineering and Other Expert Fees. The two items that comprise the $503 in the column "Not proven but possible" are expenditures for two expert witnesses named Laurel and Hardy, for $453 and $50 respectively. In the latter case, no bill was presented. In both cases, the relationship to the subject property was not proven.

3. The Architect Fee to Ms. Mimi, for $6,000, was undocumented.

4. Out of Pocket Expenses. This was an estimate by Mr. Costello for lunches, telephone expenses, miscellaneous, office, paper, etc., relating to the properties. Mr. Costello alleges that these are the normal types of expenses necessary and usual in taking a piece of property from its raw stage to a "useable" stage. It would seem a reasonable assumption that some of these expenses, if not all, did in fact occur. It is also reasonable that proof does not exist for some or all of these expenses.

5. Renovation of Existing House. Of the total $23,138 of expenses submitted by Mr. Costello, $1,664 were deemed, outright, as not relevant — that is, they are inherently personal in nature and cannot be attributed to the building. They are as follows:

   - $ 40 — The Pleasure Store — deluxe vibrator
   - $1,269 — United Electronics — large screen television
   - $ 355 — Samantha's — leather goods

In addition, $18,063 of expenses were deemed to be possible but not adequately proven. Though there were bills in support of some of these payments, the nexus with the Becka property was not proven. They are as follows:

- $ 3,345 — Caine — painting and renovation
- $ 532 — Abel — painting and wallpaper
- $ 100 — Abel — painting and wallpaper
- $ 11 — County Lighting
- $ 135 — Majors — General Contractor
- $ 1,350 — Simple — painting
- $ 525 — Simon — airconditioning and furnace
- $ 1,050 — B. Bush — landscaping
- $ 175 — O. Mission — insurance
- $ 140 — gas and water
- $ 300 — out of pocket expenses
- $10,400 — Mallory DeMer

The last item, Mr. DeMer, was an employee of Suburban Plumbing (a Company owned by Mr. Costello), and ran the operations of Fleeting Builders. Mr. Costello has attributed $200 a week for one year, totalling $10,400, of Mr. DeMer's salary for the supervision of the renovation of the house, carpentry work, and various other labor services allegedly performed by Mr. DeMer.

6. Allowance for Office, Telephone, and Secretarial. This was an estimate/ guess by Mr. Costello and his accountant as to the portion of Mr. Costello's general overhead that they felt should be assessable against the Becka property. It is questionable whether this type of an expense is legitimately chargeable to the Becka property or any other property, but it is possible. The question is, did the agreement between Costello and Abbott implicitly provide for the general overhead to be at Mr. Costello's expense?

7. Central Air Conditioning. I was shown an invoice, dated May 17, 1977, for for $3,500 for labor and material for the installation of the central air conditioning in the house at 7-11 Dispute Road in Bridgewater. This is the house on the Becka property. The bill was from Suburban Plumbing — which is owned by Mr. Costello. It is possible that indeed the house does have central air, which to a degree, has improved the value of the property. However, it does not alter the fact that the bill for $3,500 is from one of the parties in this suit.

8. Income Tax On Profit at Sale. I was shown the federal tax return of MNY, Inc. for the year ended August 31, 1978 — the year in which the Becka property was sold. The bottom line tax on this return was $15,709, for which Mr. Costello's accountant allocated 7/9th's (excluding the two lots otherwise attributable), resulting in a $12,218 federal income tax allegedly allocable to the sale of the property. I have rejected this in total inasmuch as there are several factors that complicate the situation and I don't believe that any of the tax can be attributed as a legitimate expense of the operation. My reasons include that, just as the tax on the gain might be chargeable

to the property, it follows that the tax benefit of the write-offs of expenses should be credited to the property. These expenses include, at a minimum, $47,669 of real estate taxes, $8,460 of interest on the purchase money mortgage, and various other expenses which might have been written off. It is expected, therefore, that MNY, Inc. and Mr. Costello, through various other companies, received the full tax benefit of these write-offs — roughly equivalent to the full amount of the taxable profit realized. Further, I raise the question as to whether the agreement (probably unclear in this area) provides for the charge back of income taxes.

9. My understanding of the Becka property is that the original purchase had nine useable lots with some extra land, and that Mr. Costello bought/traded with "Louie," thus giving up some money and some land, and getting in exchange, sufficient land which enabled the original Becka property to yield two more building lots. This gave the tract a total of 11 lots. Nine were sold and two are still owned. Mr. Costello alleges, and I leave it to the Court to agree or not, that the two lots attributable to the "Louie" property are not part of this deal and that their sale, at $14,250 each for a total of $28,500, does not enter into this agreement and that, therefore, Mr. Abbott is not entitled to share in such. I present to the Court that if, in fact, this is the situation, the various expenses (such as real estate taxes and interest), which apparently were for the entire property, are not all fully chargeable against Mr. Abbott's interest. Certainly, if Mr. Abbott is not entitled to share in the profit of a certain piece of property, he is not chargeable for the expenses relevant thereto.

10. As to the September 4, 1977 contract, selling nine lots at $14,250, for a total of $128,250, there were two significant adjustments to the sale that increased the price and, therefore, would either reduce the related expenses or increase the total proceeds in which Mr. Abbott and Mr. Costello could share. These two items are $1,000 labeled "Adjustment per agreement," and $1,674 that is an adjustment for real estate taxes. This latter item would reduce the real estate taxes in the schedule of expenses relating to the Becka property.

11. Engineering and Legal. The nexus to the Becka property of the following engineering and legal expenses was inadequately shown. They are as follows:

- $1,545 — Cannonball Casey — engineering
- $ 359 — Steel & Mason — legal
- $ 320 — Steel & Mason — legal

12. Landscaping and Fill. This expense was allegedly to Frank's Construction in May of 1977. No bills were presented.

13. From this total purchase and two part sale and condemnation, what remains are two vacant lots. What is the value of those two lots? Based on the illustration of costs and sales proceeds, there is at this time, between $5,000 and $10,000 of costs in excess of sales proceeds — before allowance for the value of the two remaining lots. If it is agreed that the two remaining lots have a value in the vicinity of under $10,000, then it is likely that this property has yielded no profits. If, however, it is determined that the value of these two lots is in excess of $10,000, it is likely that Mr. Abbott has some profit interest in such — though they may need be sold before he can realize such profit.

WIFE VS DOCTOR

LOVE MEDICAL ASSOCIATES

TABLE OF CONTENTS

Mr. Attorney

Re: Wife vs Doctor

Dear Mr. Attorney:

Our assignment was to analyze the operations of Love Medical Associates, and to develop sufficient financial and background data on the practice to enable a medical practice appraiser to value Doctor Fudd's interest in Love Medical Associates and his compensation therefrom. Our findings are detailed in the body of this report.

This report should not be considered as an audit in accordance with generally accepted auditing standards, but rather, an investigatory evaluation prepared for the purposes as stated above.

Very truly yours,

Kalman A. Barson, CPA
Member of the Firm

WIFE VS DOCTOR
LOVE MEDICAL ASSOCIATES
INTRODUCTION AND GENERAL COMMENTS

Love Medical Associates is a general practice medical association located in Mid-Atlantic, USA. At both dates of concern in this case — the complaint date of November 20, 1980 and the divorce decree date of November 12, 1982 — the ownership of this association was 1/3 each by Doctors Fudd, Bugs, and Duck. Dr. Duck joined the practice at the end of the 1979 fiscal year.

We performed our investigatory services on October 29 in the office of the accounting firm for Love Medical Associates. Our examination continued on October 30, at the offices of Love Medical Associates. Previous to that, and subsequent thereto, additional analysis was performed in our office.

Although Dr. Fudd was not available on Thursday, October 30 at the office of Love Medical Associates, Dr. Bugs did make himself available for questions. In addition to descriptive factors as detailed above relating to the nature of the practice, additional information relevant to this valuation was discussed.

The practice operates Monday through Friday, generally on an appointment-only basis. While walk-ins are accepted, there is a strong preference that all patients make appointments, and, in fact, there are relatively few walk-ins. Hours are 9 A.M. to 4 P.M. and 6 P.M. to 9 P.M. There are no scheduled hours on the weekends, with the three doctors alternating, each having one week out of three to be on call Friday night through Sunday. Each doctor makes rounds at the local hospital (Yosemite Medical Center) each day, four days a week, typically for 1 1/2 to 2 hours per day. In addition, the on-call doctor makes rounds Saturday and Sunday at the hospital. Dr. Bugs estimated that there are typically 15 patients per set of office hours, with each set being a three hour session. There are three such sessions per day — morning, afternoon, and evening.

A stand-out item in our discussions with Dr. Bugs and our analysis of the books and records of the practice, was that the practice enjoys relatively modest hours — there are no scheduled hours on the weekends, and the doctors generally only work an average of 35 hours per week. This modest pace was described by Dr. Bugs as being one of intent inasmuch as none of the doctors has any desire to work harder for the money. This contrasts sharply with the hours rendered by the typical general practitioner — 50 to 55 hours per week per practitioner. It is our opinion that, because of the limited hours of this practice, there are, in reality, the equivalent of only two full-time producers rather than the three doctors practicing their version of full-time work. Three doctors at 35 hours each amounts to 105 hours per week — more typically the burden of two medical practitioners.

We asked Dr. Bugs for an explanation or justification as to the practice of paying the personal residential home phone bills of all three doctors. His response was that it's a feeling of the doctors that a large part of the bills are business related. No further support is maintained in the files or elsewhere to verify such. In addition, the doctors receive reimbursement or expense allowance from the practice for automobile and entertainment expenses. No documentation or other support is rendered for same.

WIFE VS DOCTOR
LOVE MEDICAL ASSOCIATES
HOURS WORKED

To determine the number of hours worked by each doctor, we utilized the appointment cards, choosing eight weeks at random during the period July, 1980 through June, 1982.

The weeks chosen were August 11th to the 15th, 1980; October 20th to the 24th, 1980; February 2nd to the 6th, 1981; April 6th to the 10th, 1981; July 13th to the 17th, 1981; September 21st to the 25th, 1981; November 9th to the 13th, 1981; and March 15th to the 19th, 1982. We scheduled the number of hours, based on the number of sessions worked by each doctor for each of those weeks. A session is three hours – either the morning, the afternoon, or the evening.

Based on this analysis, it was determined that the doctors typically worked seven 3 hour sessions for two weeks consecutively, and six 3 hour sessions the third week. In addition, the doctors each week typically worked two hours per day for four days at the hospital – for a total of eight hours per week. This amounts to approximately 29 hours each week for two weeks, and 26 hours the third week in a three week stretch – for an average of 28 hours per week. In addition, each doctor is on call one weekend out of three. According to Dr. Bugs, the weekend duty is usually very light. We estimated six hours of actual work per weekend, which is two hours each week for each doctor, inasmuch as each doctor serves one weekend out of three. We estimated that the administrative functions of the practice occupied approximately five hours per week of each doctor's time.

Therefore, our analysis has determined that, in an average week, each doctor works as follows:

Patient Time at the office and in the hospital	28 hours
On Call Work	2 hours
Administrative	5 hours
TOTAL	35 hours

Our discussions with Dr. Bugs indicated that these abbreviated hours are at their choosing. Furthermore, as remarked to us by one of their office personnel, if they did not close the doors, patients would just keep coming in (this was in reference to the door being locked at a certain hour). Further, considering the relatively greater than average profitability, it is our opinion that the practice, to be made comparable to profession norms and expectations, should have its gross, its net, and the number of hours worked by each doctor, increased by 50%. The presentation of the operations of this practice was based on the hypothesis that it was operating as any other such medical practice would. Moreover, the presentation is intended to indicate to a potential purchaser of the practice, the volume of work and profitability that should be anticipated.

WIFE VS DOCTOR

LOVE MEDICAL ASSOCIATES

	STATEMENT OF OPERATIONS FOR THE YEARS ENDED				
	1982	1981	1980	1979	1978
	(FIGURES ROUNDED TO THE NEAREST HUNDRED $)				
GROSS INCOME	$349,100	$297,000	$301,900	$276,100	$239,400
Operating Expenses – excluding officers' compensation and retirement plan contribution	169,400	146,100	129,600	144,400	136,500
NET PROFIT – BEFORE ADJUSTMENT	179,700	150,900	172,300	131,700	102,900
Adjustments					
Petty cash – Note 1	1,000	1,000	1,000	1,000	1,000
Telephone – Note 2	1,200	1,200	1,200	1,200	1,200
Entertainment – Note 3	—	—	—	—	—
Auto expenses – Note 4	6,600	6,600	4,900	3,200	3,200
ADJUSTED NET INCOME	188,500	159,700	179,400	137,100	108,300
NET PER OFFICER	62,800	53,200	59,800	68,500	54,100
NET AS PERCENT OF GROSS	54.0%	53.8%	59.4%	49.7%	45.2%

* *

Hypothetical Potential Operations – predicated upon 50% increase in working hours (in line with profession norms).

Gross	$523,650	$445,500	$452,850	$414,150	$359,500
Gross – per officer	174,550	148,500	150,950	207,075	179,550
Net – per officer	94,200	79,800	89,700	102,750	81,150

WIFE VS DOCTOR
LOVE MEDICAL ASSOCIATES
COMPARISONS TO PROFESSION NORMS
(NOTE 5)

	LOVE MEDICAL ASSOCIATES (ACTUAL)	LOVE MEDICAL ASSOCIATES (POTENTIAL)	PROFILE OF MEDICAL PRACTICE	MEDICAL ECONOMICS
Net Income 1982	$ 60,250	$ 90,375	$ —	$ 69,020
Net Income 1981	58,000	87,000	—	63,950
Net income 1981 – Eastern U.S.	58,000	87,000	—	51,360
Net income 1980	56,500	84,750	63,300	64,860
Net income 1979	64,150	96,225	62,000	57,690
Net income 1978	61,300	91,950	54,600	53,470
Net income 1979 – Mid-Atlantic	64,150	96,225	50,200	—
Net income 1978 – Mid-Atlantic	61,300	91,950	41,400	—
Net income 1979 – Non-Metropolitan	64,150	96,225	69,200	—
Net income 1978 – Non-Metropolitan	61,300	91,950	57,700	—
Net income 1979 – 2–3 MD's Group	64,150	96,225	65,200	—
Gross Income 1982	115,870	173,800	—	125,160
Gross income 1981	107,680	161,520	—	112,880
Gross income 1981 – Eastern U.S.	107,680	161,520	—	81,110

* *

Hours worked per week 1980–1982	35	52	48.2	57
Hours worked per week 1976–1979	35	52	49.7	61
Hours per week –Mid-Atlantic – 1979–1980	35	52	47.1	–
Hour per week – Non-Metropolitan – 1979–1980	35	52	51.5	–
Hours per week – 2–3 MD's Group – 1980	35	52	52.7	–
Hours per week – Direct Patient Care – 1978–1980	30	45	45.1	–
Hours per week – Direct Patient Care – Mid-Atlantic – 1979–1980	30	45	42.5	–
Hours per week – Direct Patient Care – Non-Metropolitan – 1979–1980	30	45	48.4	–

* *

Office Visits per week – 1979–1980	83	124	118	110
Office Visits per week – 1978–1980 – Non-Metropolitan	83	124	134	–

WIFE VS DOCTOR
LOVE MEDICAL ASSOCIATES
NOTES TO REPORT

Note 1.   Petty cash — Petty cash expense typically runs approximately $90 per week. Documentation is, for the most part, adequate, though some portion of these expenses is for the personal benefit of the doctors. We have therefore attributed $20 per week of the petty cash as nonbusiness related.

Note 2.   Telephone expense. The doctors pay their personal residence telephone bills, in their entirety, through the practice. No documentation nor substantiation was offered in support of same. Accepting that some part of the telephone bills would be legitimately attributable to business, we have estimated that $100 per month of the telephone bills represent personal expenditures.

Note 3.   Entertainment. No documentation was offered for entertainment expenses. In addition, the reimbursements to the doctors were quarterly, in round amounts, and equal in amount for each doctor. However, the entertainment expense in its entirety does not appear unreasonable in light of the nature of the practice. Therefore, no adjustment has been made for this expense.

Note 4.   Auto expenses. The medical practice pays an unusually high amount of auto expenses. No documentation is offered in support of same, nor records kept that would support the business related use. Considering the type of practice, and the relatively limited need for an automobile other than for commutation, it was estimated that 50% of the auto expenses were personal in nature.

Note 5.   Comparisons to profession norms. The sources of comparison were from the American Medical Association's *Profile of Medical Practice*, the 1981 and 1980 editions; and from *Medical Economics*, the September 19, 1983, June 13, 1983, and December 20, 1982 issues. All numbers presented are averages for general practitioners, and are per practitioner.

Two columns were presented for Love Medical Associates data. The first column, labeled "actual," represents, in accordance with the adjusted net income per officer and other related figures, the *actual* results of operations. The second column, labeled "potential," reflects *hypothetical* earnings and possible performances if working hours were more akin to the average general practitioner. It would take a 50% increase in the number of hours worked per doctor to approximate national and various local averages. We applied that 50% across the board, to both net and gross income. We treated as offsets the concept that a 50% increase in gross should result in a better than 50% increase in the bottom line because of economies of scale and because various expenses are not totally variable; on the other hand, one must recognize that the increase in volume is in part hypothetical inasmuch as it has not been realized.

FLOWTHRU VS FLOWTHRU

REPORT OF FINDINGS

TABLE OF CONTENTS

PAGE

Emily Savvy, Esq.

Re: Flowthru vs Flowthru

Dear Ms. Savvy:

At your request, we expanded our services to analyze the personal financial transactions of Arthur Flowthru. Our report is, in certain respects, incomplete. We did not have access to all of the Hidden Bank cancelled checks. Neither did we have the cooperation of Arthur Flowthru — various financial records were not made available to us.

This report should not be considered as an audit in accordance with generally accepted accounting principles, but rather an investigatory evaluation prepared for the purposes of the determination of the conclusions detailed herein.

Very truly yours,

Kalman A. Barson, CPA
Member of the Firm

FLOWTHRU VS FLOWTHRU

ANALYSIS OF ARTHUR FLOWTHRU'S PERSONAL CHECKING ACCOUNTS

AUGUST 1977 THROUGH 1982

Checks Payable to Cash

There were frequent and recurring checks, ranging up to the several hundred dollar level, drawn to cash. This by itself is not unusual. However, there were recurring patterns of the endorsements on the back of these checks that are noteworthy. The following is a brief analysis of the magnitude of checks payable to cash that were endorsed by Miss Matic, a known coin dealer:

1977 (after August)	4 checks	$ 1,675
1978	12	3,255
1979	23	6,549
1980	20	4,629
1981	6	4,525
1982	1	575
Total of the above	66 checks	$21,208

The magnitude and frequency of the cash checks endorsed by Miss Matic suggests that they were used to buy coins.

Checks Payable to Gas Companies — Gas Credit Cards

During testimony, the issue of the personal auto expenses of Mr. Flowthru was raised. He indicated that he had two gas credit cards, and that he used them for his personal gas expenditures. The following is an analysis of payments to gas companies for the years covered:

1977	1 check		$ 10.00
1978	1 check		11.50
1979	2 checks	$ 80.65	
		1.04	
			81.69
1980	3 checks	13.40	
		12.30	
		20.50	
			46.20
1981	1 check		20.00
1982	No checks		—
Six-year total	8 checks		$169.39

A negligible amount of gasoline expense was incurred and paid by Mr. Flowthru personally over a six-year period.

Auto Maintenance

For the six-year period, the following is an analysis of the checks paid to auto dealers or repair shops on behalf of auto maintenance:

- 1977:   none
- 1978:   none
- 1979:   2 checks: one each in September and November; for $23.00 and $7.95, respectively, a total of $30.95.
- 1980:   6 checks: one each in February, May, August, September, November, and December, for $339.96, $21.10, $200.00, $157.16, $50.00, and $53.00, respectively, for a total of $821.22.
- 1981:   4 checks: one each in February, June, July, and August; for $90.39, $25.52, $28.87, and $68.37, respectively; for a total of $213.15.
- 1982:   2 checks: one each in August and September; for $10.07 and $249.98, respectively; for a total of $260.05.
- The six-year total: $1,325.37.

Utility Bills

The following is an analysis of water, telephone, electric/gas, and heating oil bills paid through the personal checking accounts of Mr. Flowthru from 1978 through 1982.

YEAR	WATER $	WATER AVG/MO	TELEPHONE $	TELEPHONE AVG/MO	ELECTRIC/GAS $	ELECTRIC/GAS AVG/MO	OIL $	OIL AVG/MO
1978	$ 78	$ 7	$2,600	$217	$1,263	$105	$1,816	$151
1979	63	5	1,221	102	1,571	131	1,659	138
1980	138	12	367	31	1,423	119	2,302	184
1981	160	13	339	28	1,261	105	–0–	–0–
1982	165	14	384	32	1,536	128	–0–	–0–

The above illustrates the modest amount for utility bills paid personally by Mr. Flowthru. We had been advised that he has extremely high oil bills because of his large house. In fact, we found that for 1981 and 1982 he paid no oil bills through his personal accounts. However, we do know that Flowthru Products Company paid a significant number of fuel oil bills.

Legal Bills

The following is a detailing of the legal bills paid by Mr. Flowthru through his personal checking accounts.

MONTH/YEAR	PAYEE	AMOUNT
October 1978	Underling	$ 200.00
January 1979	Overling	1,333.87
March 1979	Ling-Ling	500.00
June 1979	Hop	308.80
December 1979	Skip	192.00
December 1979	Jump	20.00
1980		—
1981		—
1982		—
Five-year total		$2,554.67

The above indicates that in the five-year period 1978–1982, Mr. Flowthru personally paid a total of $2,554.67 in legal bills. This was during a period when there were significant legal proceedings in matrimonial and other areas affecting Mr. Flowthru. The vast bulk of his legal expenses were paid by Flowthru Products Company.

Internal Revenue Service

In addition to the preceeding, on July 4, 1980, Mr. Flowthru drew a check for $10,000, from his Hidden Bank account, payable to the IRS. This check cannot be accounted for from his known/supplied tax returns. Similarly, an August, 1979 check for $14,786.33, payable to the IRS cannot be accounted for from the tax returns.

FLOWTHRU VS FLOWTHRU
MATTERS RELEVANT TO THE BANK ACCOUNTS
OF ARTHUR FLOWTHRU

We repeatedly requested copies of all the bank statements (checking and savings) and other indicia of savings of Mr. Flowthru. On January 16, 1983, the Court instructed Mr. Flowthru to submit such records to us. We were supplied with records relevant to just two checking accounts: the joint checking account of Arthur and Alice Flowthru at First Regional Bank, #02–007–0000; and the checking account of Arthur Flowthru at First Infidelity National Bank, #02–007–0069. Despite the existence of savings and/or certificate of deposit interest income on the tax returns of Mr. Flowthru, no records relevant to such were produced. Furthermore, investigation of the endorsements on the back of various joint account checks indicated the existence of at least one other account: #0812345 at First Regional Bank in the name of Arthur Flowthru; and the possible existence of another account in Hidden Bank.

The following is a listing of checks drawn by Mr. Flowthru against the joint account, the disposition or use of which we have been unable to ascertain based on records made available to date.

#519	10/24/78	A.F.	$ 5,000
544	10/1/80	Cash	16,800
532	12/21/80	Cash	33,600
547	3/14/81	Cash	48,325
546	4/11/81	Cash	100,000
548	5/6/81	Cash	16,800
550	6/27/81	Cash	25,200
551	10/1/81	Cash	25,200
553	12/22/81	Cash	33,600
554	3/12/82	Cash	200,000
555	4/6/82	Cash	70,000

The above represents $574,525 of checks drawn by Arthur Flowthru out of funds owned jointly with Alice Flowthru, all but $5,000 payable to "cash," the use of which has not been explained.

It should be further explained that the above referenced joint account was in the sole possession of Mr. Flowthru, and, from 1978 through 1982, the only transactions therein were the depositing of joint distribution checks by Mr. Flowthru, and the simultaneous withdrawal of same, by Mr. Flowthru — by checks payable either to himself or to cash.

The following is a listing of deposits, of $10,000 or more, to Mr. Flowthru's account #007–0069 at First Infidelity, the sources of which we have been unable to deduce:

1/9/79	$ 22,500
3/14/79	93,769
4/3/79	10,000
6/30/79	20,100
4/16/80	108,145
7/24/80	12,000
5/1/82	253,138

The following is an incomplete listing, derived from the incomplete copies of statements of Mr. Flowthru's account #007–0069 at First Infidelity, of checks of $10,000 or more, drawn on that account, the use of which we have been unable to deduce:

4/27/78	$ 10,002
3/16/80	130,000
5/4/80	95,941
7/27/80	10,000
8/8/80	10,800
3/18/82	18,850
5/1/82	86,554

FLOWTHRU VS FLOWTHRU
TAX RETURNS OF ARTHUR FLOWTHRU
1978–1982

Months after we requested, we were supplied with alleged copies of Mr. Flowthru's tax returns for 1978 through 1982. We found that these returns raised a number of issues compelling enough to request authenticated, certified copies directly from the Internal Revenue Service. We have not yet been granted authorization to so obtain these returns. These and other issues include:

1. In a few instances, whether it be for the Federal or State returns, a copy of the check in payment of the tax balance was attached. These attached checks have a number of apparent or potential defects as follows:

   A. They are unnumbered.
   B. There are no visible cancellation marks from the bank.
   C. We cannot find some of these checks on the partially submitted bank statements of Arthur Flowthru. The checks in payment of the 1979 and 1980 Federal and State Tax Returns do not appear on the checking account statements supplied to us.

2. Despite his salary of over $100,000 a year and total income ranging from $300,000 to over $500,000 a year in each of the years 1978 through 1982, his income from sources other than Flowthru Products never exceed $1,000 and, in fact, in 1981 there was no other income.

3. The returns show an extremely high level of sales tax deducted each year. That indicates that he has spent, on items subject to sales tax, well over $100,000, and often close to $200,000, per year, consistently over the last few years.

4. The returns were missing certain key schedules — indicated on the return as being attached, yet not submitted to us.

5. There are various inconsistencies in the typing and reproducing quality of the returns submitted; the 1981 return was handwritten whereas the returns for other years were typed; there are some (minor) arithmetic errors on the returns; we cannot reconcile the deduction for state and local income taxes to known information; the typing on the 1979 Form 3468 is different than the typing on the rest of the return.

FLOWTHRU VS FLOWTHRU

RECONSTRUCTION OF INCOME AND EXPENDITURES OF ARTHUR FLOWTHRU

1978–1982

	1978	1979	1980	1981	1982
INCOME – PER TAX RETURNS					
Salary – Flowthru Products	$100,710	$122,736	$119,360	$140,853	$114,168
Interest income	937	450	342	—	3,000
Distributions from Flowthru					
Products	197,934	244,770	245,568	441,439	—
Less: distributions received					
following year	(113,089)	(148,970)	(161,569)	(349,089)	(—)
Add: previous year's distri-					
bution received	56,152	113,089	148,970	161,569	349,089
Miscellaneous	—	6,800	1,875	3,600	38
TOTAL KNOWN/					
ADMITTED INCOME	242,644	338,875	354,546	398,546	466,295
RECONSTRUCTION OF					
EXPENDITURES					
Stock purchase – Flowthru					
Products	—	23,920	—	—	—
Personal (pocket money) –					
Note 1	6,387	7,514	8,840	10,400	11,960
Food – Note 2	5,142	6,049	7,117	8,373	9,850
Home and lawn maintenance					
– Note 2	5,377	6,325	7,442	8,755	10,300
Utilities (electric, gas, and oil)					
– Note 2	3,320	3,906	4,595	5,406	6,360
Telephone – Note 2	656	729	810	900	1,000
Sundries – Note 1	2,211	2,601	3,060	3,600	4,140
Auto expense – Note 3	—	—	—	—	—
Clothes – Note 2	7,873	8,748	9,720	10,800	12,000
Gifts and entertainment – Note 3	—	—	—	—	—
Contributions – Note 4	5,805	6,162	7,590	8,647	4,167
Federal and State taxes – Note 4	135,560	164,402	177,061	358,171	54,038
Less taxes paid following					
year – Note 4	(88,080)	(108,880)	(112,297)	(286,554)	—
Add previous year's tax paid					
– Note 4	83,452	88,080	108,880	112,297	286,554
Real estate taxes – Note 4	1,745	1,856	1,739	1,851	2,104
Mortgage Interest – Note 4	2,097	2,097	2,494	3,809	2,889
Vacations – Note 2	5,249	5,832	6,480	7,200	8,000
Tangible personal property ac-					
quisitions subject to sales					
tax – Note 5	123,367	164,967	236,433	152,550	119,367
Tangible personal property ac-					
quisitions – out-of-state					
–Note 6	9,104	21,682	71,392	81,958	49,539

FLOWTHRU VS FLOWTHRW (CONT.)
RECONSTRUCTION OF INCOME AND EXPENDITURES OF ARTHUR FLOWTHRU
1978–1982

	1978	1979	1980	1981	1982
Child care expenses – Note 4	1,037	2,300	—	—	—
Other interest – Note 4	6,562	7,073	6,881	4,556	3,977
Miscellaneous deductions – Note 4	7,639	17,024	16,723	1,265	1,667
Payments to acquire Proctology Associates	33,333	33,333	33,333	33,333	33,333
Mortgage principal payments –Note 7	4,779	4,779	4,382	3,067	3,683
Insurance – Note 2	4,461	4,957	5,508	6,120	6,800
TOTAL EXPENDITURES	367,076	475,456	608,183	536,504	631,728
INCOME (DEFICIENCY)	$(124,432)	$(136,581)	$(253,637)	$(138,132)	$(165,433)

SUMMARY FOR 1978 THROUGH 1982:

Total income	$1,800,732
Total expenditures	2,618,947
Income (Deficiency)	$ (818,215)

FLOWTHRU VS FLOWTHRU

NOTES TO RECONSTRUCTION OF INCOME AND EXPENDITURES
OF ARTHUR FLOWTHRU

SUMMATION: This schedule suggests possible irregularities or unknowns. It would appear that Mr. Flowthru has other sources of funds not revealed to us.

NOTE 1.   Personal and sundries — These items were estimated for 1981, and reduced successively by 15% for each year prior, up to and including 1978; and increased by 15% for 1982.

NOTE 2.   Food, home and lawn maintenance, utilities, telephone, clothes, vacations, and insurance — These items for 1982 were taken directly from Arthur Flowthru's expense budget statement, submitted in this present action, and reduced successively by 15% per year (for food, home and lawn maintenance, and utilities) and by 10% per year (for telephone, clothes, vacations, and insurance) for the years 1981– 1978.

NOTE 3.   Auto and gifts and entertainment — These items were not on Mr. Flowthru's budget and, therefore, were treated as being paid in total by the Company.

NOTE 4.   Contributions, taxes, interest, child care, and miscellaneous deductions —These items were taken directly from Mr. Flowthru's tax returns.

NOTE 5.   Tangible property — Based on the sales tax deducted on Mr. Flowthru's tax returns, after reducing same by a $300 annual allowance for sales tax on normal and customary living needs, we calculated what had to be spent on asset acquisitions to warrant such substantial sales tax deductions.   Inasmuch as Mr. Flowthru's testimony included that he pays no sales tax on out-of-state purchases, we used his home state's sales tax rate for this procedure.   Such purchases might include, for example, furniture, antiques, precious metals and jewels, furs, and various other collectibles for investment.

NOTE 6.   Tangible property (out-of-state) — Based on our incomplete analysis of Mr. Flowthru's checking accounts, to the extent expenditures were known to have been made out-of-state, and based on Mr. Flowthru's testimony that he does not pay sales tax on out-of-state purchases, such out-of-state purchases would be in addition to purchases derived from grossing up the expenditures necessary to generate the sales tax deductions presented on his tax returns. Inasmuch as we did not have all the cancelled checks, it is probable that this expense was somewhat greater.

NOTE 7.   Mortgage Principal — Based on Mr. Flowthru's budget, after reductions of real estate taxes and mortgage interest as per his tax returns.

INDEX

INDEX